Michael,

Thanks for your Friendship,
and your partnership.

My best

MORE THAN MONEY

Since 1996, Bloomberg Press has published books for financial professionals on investing, economics, and policy affecting investors. Titles are written by leading practitioners and authorities, and have been translated into more than 20 languages.

The Bloomberg Financial Series provides both core reference knowledge and actionable information for financial professionals. The books are written by experts familiar with the work flows, challenges, and demands of investment professionals who trade the markets, manage money, and analyze investments in their capacity of growing and protecting wealth, hedging risk, and generating revenue.

For a list of available titles, please visit our website at www.wiley.com/go/bloombergpress.

MORE THAN MONEY

A Guide to Sustaining Wealth and
Preserving the Family

Michael A. Cole

WILEY

Published by John Wiley & Sons, Inc., Hoboken, New Jersey.Published simultaneously in Canada.

For general information on our other products and services or for technical support, please contact our Customer Care Department within the United States at (800) 762–2974, outside the United States at (317) 572–3993 or fax (317) 572–4002.

Wiley publishes in a variety of print and electronic formats and by print-on-demand. Some material included with standard print versions of this book may not be included in e-books or in print-on-demand. If this book refers to media such as a CD or DVD that is not included in the version you purchased, you may download this material at http://booksupport.wiley.com. For more information about Wiley products, visit www.wiley.com.

Library of Congress Cataloging-in-Publication Data is available:

ISBN 978-1-119-26470-5 (Hardcover)
ISBN 978-1-119-26473-6 (epdf)
ISBN 978-1-119-26480-4 (epub)

Cover Design: Wiley

Printed in the United States of America

10 9 8 7 6 5 4 3 2 1

MIX
Paper from
responsible sources
FSC® C014174

Dedicated to my son Daniel, whose time with us was cut way too short yet his impact was larger than life itself. Life is about so much more than money, and I would give any amount to have him back.

Contents

Preface   ix

Acknowledgments   xi

About the Author   xiii

PART I: THE MEANING OF WEALTH

CHAPTER 1
The Wealth Management Challenge   3

CHAPTER 2
Wealth Is More Than Money   11

CHAPTER 3
The Impact of Wealth Stewardship   25

PART II: UNDERSTANDING THE WEALTH MANAGEMENT PROCESS

CHAPTER 4
The Importance of Integrating Tactical and Strategic Wealth
Management   41

CHAPTER 5
Should We Manage Wealth as a Family?   51

CHAPTER 6
The Story of Wealth Creation: Why It Matters   61

CHAPTER 7
Vision and Mission: The Past, the Present, and the Future   71

CHAPTER 8
**Family Governance: Roles and Responsibilities, Decision
Making, and Conflict Resolution**

81

CHAPTER 9
Developing Future Leadership

103

CHAPTER 10
**Family Education: Building a Culture of Learning
and Continuous Improvement**

113

CHAPTER 11
**Communication and Alignment: Working Together
as a High-Functioning Team**

123

CHAPTER 12
Integrating Tactical Wealth Management

131

CHAPTER 13
Getting It Right

145

Index

157

Preface

Creating substantial financial resources requires a combination of skill, luck, and timing. Very few people are successful at creating and accumulating wealth that provides more than what is necessary to maintain their standard of living and sustain them throughout their lives. A gifted, fortunate few build levels of wealth that have the potential to last well beyond their lifetime and create impact far beyond their earthly existence.

For these fortunate few, it is an incredible gift and a substantial burden to enjoy, manage, transfer, and sustain the fortunes they have created or inherited. Several studies document the fact that 70 percent of the time significant wealth evaporates by the third generation. In addition, only 12 percent of family businesses are still in operation by the third generation. How many successful entrepreneurs think of the business they created as their legacy that will survive over time and generations? The fact is only one in nine family businesses survives the test of time and succession.

If these unique and exceptionally talented individuals and families have been so successful in creating great wealth, then why are so many of them failing at long-term wealth management and sustainability? Is it poor investment performance, inadequate tax planning, ineffective legal structuring, or substandard advice? Certainly, all these aspects play a part in the preservation of wealth over time. However, extensive research demonstrates that 95 percent of the failures are due to other causes, including poor communication and lack of trust among family members, inadequate preparation of the next generation, and the absence of a shared mission or vision among the family.

Families that have accumulated great wealth are still families and interact with each other based on emotions, including love, passion, anger, resentment, jealousy, and fear. Yet, given the wealth they have created, they also often display many of the characteristics of operating businesses, such as centralized management, shareholders, and employees. They have family leaders, who are the equivalent of the management team; they have family stakeholders, who are equivalent to shareholders; and they have family members and nonfamily members who work in the business of running and managing the family. These people are the equivalent of employees.

The challenge that the larger majority of wealthy families face is that they do not take a strategic approach to the business of family wealth management. They tend to be tactical, focusing on the core, traditional wealth management issues such as investment management, tax planning, estate planning, and cash flow management. All of these aspects are critically important, but by themselves they will not provide for successful wealth management and positive wealth impact throughout multiple generations.

The focus on this book is to provide families the view of their wealth as more than money and to take a strategic approach to managing wealth and the impact that it has on the people and issues that matter to them most. It is not intended as a deep technical guide. Instead, it provides a high-level overview of strategic processes and basic tools for consideration. It also provides stories of families I have had the pleasure to work with over the last thirty years. Each story is an amalgamation of several families to illustrate the challenges and opportunities that come with managing resources effectively as a family enterprise. From the families I have consulted with throughout my career, I have learned as much as if not more than I have been able to give to them.

Acknowledgments

When I was first approached to write a book, I gave it considerable thought and finally came to the conclusion that it was too important an opportunity to pass up and I really did have something meaningful to communicate. However, given that I had never done it before, I had no idea how difficult a process it is to complete. It takes shifting one's mindset out of the day-to-day "bits and bytes" of the modern world and focusing so you can deliver your message in a profound and effective way. Although a lot of the actual work is done alone, I could not have taken on or accomplished this endeavor without a lot of help and support.

I want to start by thanking my writing partner, Gretchen Hirsch. Not only is she an exquisite and creative writer, she has the most positive attitude of anyone I know. During the process of writing the book, she dealt with some significant personal challenges that would have caused most people to quit. Gretchen is just not most people. She is a cut above, and a consummate professional. This book would never have been completed without her.

Along with Gretchen, I need to acknowledge and thank my support system, which mostly includes my amazing family. The people who read this book will likely do so because they want insights about managing wealth. However, the foundation of the book is really about family, and my family provides the foundation of my existence. They give me the ability to try things, and even if I fail, I know that they will still be there for me no matter what.

It starts with my two amazing children, Daniel and Ellie. Although, at the age of sixteen, they are far beyond anything that I could learn from the parenting manual and at times push me beyond my limits, they give me much more than they can ever appreciate or understand. I love them completely and could not imagine my life without them.

Along with my two children, my love, Alicia, encourages me to seek the best of every day and live with passion and joy and be present so that I do not miss a moment. I love her spirit and am so fortunate that our paths came to be one.

My mother, Gloria, has been my greatest fan since the day I was conceived, and she is unwavering in her support of me even when it is unwarranted. She also inspires me in so many ways, including as a writer, a journalist, a feminist, a mother, a grandmother, a friend, and a believer in the possible—or sometimes the impossible.

My two sisters, Loren and Suzy, are truly the core of my foundation. More than anyone else, their commitment to family, to me, and to each other provides the inspiration for this book. They made me appreciate and realize that a strong family bond can withstand adversity, pain, and anger, and rise above it and provide strength, hope, commitment, belief, and joy. I am so proud of both of them for who they are and the wonderful families they have created and continue to foster. Due to them, we have remained a very tight-knit family. I am so honored by and proud of all my nieces and nephews, including Becca, Jake, Ben, Elijah, and Madeline. As they have grown into capable young adults, I am confident that the next generation of the Cole family will have a "wealth" of wonderful family experiences and will make the world a better place.

I also want to thank my cousin John. He is my brother from another mother. His compassion, creativity, and commitment to family above all else helps me stay focused and true and that has motivated me to stay on course in my life and my career.

In addition to my family, I need to acknowledge all of the terrific team members and partners I have the incredible honor and pleasure of working with every day at Ascent and at US Bank. The Ascent leadership team is the best in the industry. Through their incredible work and the efforts of the other members of the Ascent family, they are changing the wealth management industry for the better and helping great families do great things for themselves, their family members, and their society. In my mind, nothing could be a nobler calling.

I would like to also thank and acknowledge the incredible support I have received from the US Bank Executive Leadership team. In particular, my friend, my leader, and my mentor, Mark Jordahl, has created the environment that allows me to develop and grow as I never could have done under another leader. Along with Mark, Richard Davis, Andy Cecere, and Terry Dolan provided unwavering support, which has been amazing in an effort to complete this project.

There are many other people who have guided, inspired, and motivated me. There just is not enough space to cover them all. Nevertheless, this book is a product of all of the influences and events that have touched my life and my career, and they all have their place in this journey.

About the Author

As the president and founder of Ascent Private Capital Management of US Bank, Michael Cole is fulfilling one of his family's core values.

"My parents taught me and my two sisters that we are all citizens of a larger planet and that we needed to look for ways to give back," Cole said from his San Francisco office. "For me, the greatest way to give back is to empower people who have great wealth to use their resources—both financial and personal—to do great things for themselves and their families, live great lives, and make a positive impact on the planet."

Through Ascent Private Capital Management, Cole and his team provide ultra-high-net-worth clients with a unique and distinctive suite of wealth-management services that combine traditional wealth management offerings—financial planning, investment consulting, financial administration, private banking, trust, and estate services—with cutting-edge "wealth impact" services that help some of the country's wealthiest families with governance, risk management, education, stewardship, family leadership, and communication.

Ascent, since its creation in 2010, has won numerous industry awards and recognition, including:

- *Private Asset Management* magazine's 2014 Best Private Wealth Manager—Client Service
- *Private Asset Management* magazine's 2014 Best Private Client Investment Platform—Client Service
- *Private Asset Management* magazine's 2015 Best Multi-Family Office Service Provider
- *Private Asset Management* magazine's 2016 Best-in-Class: Private Banking Client Service
- Family Wealth Report Awards 2014 Best Brand Launch
- Family Wealth Report Awards 2016 Best Alternative Asset Manager
- *Bloomberg Markets* magazine's Annual Family Office World Ranking—2nd Fastest Growing in 2012, 5th Fastest Growing in 2013, 5th Fastest Growing in 2014

A Student of Success

From the time that he was a twenty-three-year-old financial advisor selling pensions and employee benefits to wealthy businessmen in the New York City area, Cole has been a student of success. "I learned early that 'knowledge is power' and that I needed to learn everything there was to know about my work—from the technical side of the business to rapport with people," Cole said. "I also learned what it took to succeed and what the activities were that led to success."

Cole was such a student of success that when he was only thirty-five, Merrill Lynch named him president of Merrill Lynch Trust after working at the firm for just two years. He then went on to even greater professional success at Wells Fargo, where he held senior wealth management positions and was selected to build, develop, and serve as national director of the Family Wealth Group and the Wealth Planning Center at Wells Fargo. The Family Wealth Group, which was subsequently rebranded as Abbott Downing, is now one of the largest multifamily offices in the United States.

Today, Cole spends the majority of his time sharing his vision of how Ascent Private Capital Management can help families with exceptional net worth act strategically to make an impact with their wealth. "I believe there is no higher calling than to help people move forward in a direction that creates a positive change in how they manage their wealth and impact the world," he said.

Cole also spends a great deal of time interacting with clients and working with his team. He prides himself on knowing how to hire great people and empower them to execute his vision. "My management style is to have fun and be passionate," he said. "I find it exceptionally rewarding and challenging to work with clients and team members in a business where you interface with interesting, successful people who have the resources and abilities to do amazing things."

Cole earned a bachelor's degree from Emory University in Atlanta, Georgia. He is also a Certified Financial Planner and holds Series 7, 9, 10, and 66 licenses from the NASD.

Cole resides in Los Gatos, California, with his family.

MORE THAN MONEY

PART I

The Meaning of Wealth

CHAPTER 1

The Wealth Management Challenge

The United States has always been the land of opportunity. Nearly anyone with a good idea and considerable drive can find a way to begin a business, nurture it, watch it grow, and hope to pass it on to children and grandchildren. In fact, it's estimated that 80 percent of American businesses are closely held or family enterprises the owners have built for themselves and succeeding generations.

How many of today's entrepreneurs put their names on the door and expect the business to fail? Probably none, but if they were to return to Earth within two generations, in most cases they would find that not only was the family name gone from the door, but also that the business itself had failed. According to a 2012 *Harvard Business Review* article by George Stalk Jr. and Henry Foley, "Avoid the Traps That Can Destroy Family Businesses," 70 percent of family-owned businesses, which hold the entrepreneurial founders' hopes for their families' futures, will be gone by the third generation. Most of them will fail or be sold before the second generation takes over, and only 10 percent will function as privately held companies by the third generation. The dreams of family legacy will be faint memories, perhaps preserved only in old newspaper clippings or pictures tossed into a shoebox.

The adage "Shirtsleeves to shirtsleeves in three generations" became a well-known prophecy because it is, unfortunately, true. And it appears to be true in virtually every culture. In Ireland, the saying is, "Clogs to clogs in three generations." In Italy, it's, "Stable to stars to stable" in the same time frame. In Japan, "The third generation ruins the house." The Chinese proverb is, "From paddy to paddy in three generations." Brazilians say, "Rich father, noble son, poor grandson."

3

What it often means is that the first generation works hard to build the wealth and a better life for the family; the second generation, which has known both the frugality required to make a fortune and the advantages wealth confers, understands the value of hard work and either maintains or even expands the family's assets. The third generation, which has never struggled, is less likely to see the relationship between work and reward and more likely to spend down the money—and the cycle must begin again.

Consider, for example, the Vanderbilts, who are the poster family for the diminishment of wealth. It's a well-known cautionary tale. The first-generation patriarch, Cornelius Vanderbilt, took a $100 loan from his mother and built it into a $100 million fortune by the time he died in 1877. It's reported that the money he left to his family was more than the United States government held in its Treasury at the time. In the second generation, William Henry Vanderbilt, who died only eight years after his father, doubled the family fortune to an amount equivalent to $300 billion in today's economy.

But by the third generation, the Vanderbilts abandoned the wealth-creation strategies of Cornelius and William and began a cycle of spending more than they were creating. The four sons of William Henry spent fortunes on some of the most imposing dwellings in the country. Cornelius Vanderbilt II constructed a 154-room home—the largest private residence in New York—on West 58th Street. Next came The Breakers, a seventy-room "cottage" in Newport, Rhode Island. This Italian Renaissance palazzo was modeled on those of sixteenth-century Italy and was crammed with priceless antiques and art.

Cornelius's brother, William K. Vanderbilt, also built a summer home in Newport: Marble House. According to the Preservation Society of Newport County, Marble House was inspired by the Petit Trianon at Versailles and cost $11 million, $7 million of which were spent on 500,000 cubic feet of marble.

Frederick William Vanderbilt, the most private of the brothers, built an imposing mansion at Hyde Park, with furnishings purchased from Napoleon Bonaparte's Malmaison Palace.

And in Asheville, North Carolina, the youngest of the four brothers, George Washington Vanderbilt, erected his country home, the Biltmore, America's largest private estate, which contains 250 rooms and features extensive grounds and gardens. At the time George owned the property, it comprised 125,000 acres—the size of several American townships combined. Today the property encompasses 8,000 acres, but the gardens, outbuildings, and the house itself remain almost beyond belief in their scope and attractiveness.

The lifestyles of the family members, which also included top-of-the-line yachts, horses, and other expensive pastimes, were as lavish as the family's residences (ten of them on New York's 5th Avenue). Their excessive spending came at the cost of mortgaging the family's financial future.

As Michael Klepper and Robert Gunther point out in their book, *The Wealthy 100*, by the time of the first Vanderbilt family reunion in 1973, less than a century after Cornelius Vanderbilt's death, there was not a single millionaire among the 120 members of the descendants in attendance.[1] The family was spending, but as later generations married, had children, and increased the size of the Vanderbilt clan, no one was rebuilding the fortune. They had forgotten an important lesson: As a previous generation passes away, the next generation becomes the first generation, responsible for maintaining and increasing the fortune for the growing family. That didn't happen, and it was a recipe for disaster. The wealth was static, the family was dynamic, and the Vanderbilts didn't recover.

Today, some of the family, such as Gloria Vanderbilt and her son, Anderson Cooper, are highly successful, but their current affluence comes from their work in art, fashion, and media rather than as a result of inheritance, much of which was eaten up in lawsuits that took place when Gloria was a child.

In the early days of the Vanderbilt dynasty, it's possible the family believed the sheer size of their holdings protected them from any untoward outcomes, so spending was unabated. However, most families, even those with substantial wealth, are aware that if they don't plan well, an end point is possible. In fact, if they fail to plan, they are unknowingly planning to fail.

Of course, successful wealth transition involves careful financial planning that encompasses such factors as tax and investment strategies, asset management, information management and reporting, and the consequences of growth as successive generations marry and have children, to name a few. None of these factors exists in a vacuum. Everything from climate change to regional wars to a technological crash may affect investments and financial planning, and a failure to appreciate risks and rewards can have significant deleterious effects on the maintenance of a family's wealth.

However, in their book, *Preparing Heirs: Five Steps to the Successful Transition of Family Wealth*, Roy Williams and Vic Preisser show that even the best tactical planning is not enough. Their research with more than 3,000 families over a period of twenty-five years demonstrated that:

- *60 percent* of unsuccessful wealth transitions could be traced to a breakdown of communication and trust within the family.
- *25 percent* were caused by inadequate preparation of the heirs.
- Only *15 percent* were brought about by all other causes, and of those, only *3 percent* had to do with professional failures in accounting, legal, financial, and tax advice. The rest usually could be chalked up to the family's failure to have a family wealth mission or consensus.[2]

Families with great wealth are still families. Like other families, they may interact with one another based on emotions such as love, passion, resentment, anger, jealousy, and fear. And even if most of the family members get along well, money problems can create bad feelings, ranging from spats and squabbles to intrafamily lawsuits.

The Robbie family is a case in point. Prior to his death in 1990, Joe Robbie, one-time owner of the Miami Dolphins and the stadium in which the team played, made serious estate planning blunders. Although he had trust documents in place and everything appeared to be in order, problems arose. The trust was to receive the proceeds of his estate and provide income for his wife, Elizabeth, as long as she lived.

However, most of Robbie's estate consisted of nonliquid assets that didn't provide enough money for his widow. She therefore decided to ask for the 30 percent of her husband's $70 million estate to which she was entitled under Florida law.

In forgoing the trust income to take her percentage, she triggered millions of dollars in estate taxes. Since there was insufficient cash to pay the taxes, the team and stadium had to be sold to settle the debt of approximately $45 million. Discord arose before and during the sale, and the heirs, many of whom already were at war with one another, lost the legacy their father had created and the chance for an amicable wealth transfer. Tactical planning had failed, and the family was fractured. Had Robbie attended to the more strategic aspects of the management of his estate, things might have been very different. As the family discovered, adding dollars to an already unstable relationship can be like adding gasoline to a fire. Smoldering resentments can burst into flame and the resulting conflagration may burn the house down.

The challenge most wealthy families face is that they do not take an integrated approach to family wealth management—an approach that incorporates both a strategic outlook and exceptional tactical performance. Families like the Robbies, who concentrate too heavily on traditional wealth management, generally do not do well in preparing for long-term wealth impact.

Conversely, other families may miss wealth-creating opportunities because they put too much emphasis on harmony and don't question actions and decisions made by other family members who seem to be in charge. Or they simply rock along, content with today's gains and thinking little about the future. By giving scant attention to interpersonal dynamics and communication, these families may set themselves up for failure when the economy takes a turn or a family member makes a unilateral and spectacularly bad investment decision. Furthermore, the traditional providers of wealth management services such as banks, brokerage firms, registered investment advisors, insurance agents, accountants, and attorneys focus primarily on traditional wealth and estate planning and neglect to address the strategic issues that account for 97 percent of the reasons families fail to sustain wealth. What is needed for multigenerational wealth management and sustainability is the amalgamation of both strategic and tactical planning and execution. The families who have been the most successful in running the family business also put the same kind of effort into managing the business of family.

Along with the traditional wealth management responsibilities, these families continually mine the nonfinancial elements that affect the growth (or loss) of the family enterprise. These issues include:

- *Family history and values:* Who are we as a family? What lessons can we learn from the wealth creators or the concept of wealth creation? How did our forebears build the family fortune? What do they have to teach this generation? Do we have the same values they did, or have we developed a different moral compass? Do we as a family share multigenerational values? If so, what are they?
- *Family vision and mission planning:* What do we stand for as a family? Do we have shared vision or purpose for the wealth and the family into the future? What matters to us? What do we want our family legacy to be? Do we agree? If not, how do we resolve differences of opinion about what we want our legacy to look like?
- *Communication planning:* How do we currently communicate with one another? Does that method work or should we develop new modes of communication? How can we continue to improve communication between and across generations? Would we as a family benefit from a more consistent and formal communication process?
- *Family governance:* Should we manage our wealth as a unit or should we divide and manage it independently? Right now, who's handling the wealth on behalf of the family; that is, who has the greatest say in how wealth is developed and used? Is this the most effective way to carry out the family's mission and values? What are the rights and responsibilities of each family member? Are they clearly understood and communicated? How do we ensure individual family member accountability while allowing for expedited decision making?
- *Leadership development and assistance:* How do we prepare the next generation of leaders? What skills do we need, and how do we identify who has them? What education and training should the family provide for those who will fulfill major responsibilities in the future?
- *Role clarification:* What roles currently are being played by various family members? Are there gaps we need to fill? Do we need additional members to assume new roles? How do we determine which family members are best suited for which roles? Do any roles conflict with one another? Are there roles that served us well in the past but that now can be pruned as we look to the future?

- *Family education:* How do we develop an ongoing educational program designed to prepare and train family members to successfully manage and steward wealth on behalf of themselves and the family? Should such education be carried out by the family, by other advisors, or by a combination of experts both inside and outside the family?
- *Risk:* How do we balance risk and reward? How can we avoid the risks that might undermine the family mission? How do we deal with risk if it threatens our values? How does the family priority rank and manage risks based on the likelihood of specific types of occurrences and the level of impact they would have on the family?

Using a process that is clear, well-communicated, and well-orchestrated increases a family's opportunity for long-term cooperation and unity, generational understanding and happiness, and financial prosperity.

This book helps readers answer the vital questions above and discover ways to integrate strategic and tactical wealth management tools in planning for successful wealth building and generational transfer.

MULTIGENERATIONAL BUSINESSES ARE STILL GOING STRONG. HOW DO THEY DO IT?

A big name and a huge fortune do not ensure the continuation of the family enterprise. The family name may remain on the business and the heirs represented on the board, but the founder's vision can be diluted if the family steps away from the leading roles. The table below names some businesses that have found a way to pass a family legacy from generation to generation. Family members are still active in the businesses, and these companies have grown, changed, and adapted with the times. It appears they have planned well on every front, both strategic and tactical.

Family	Business/Year Founded	Generations
Zildjian Family	Cymbals/1623 (United States in 1929)	15
Hicks Family	Plant nurseries/landscape design/1853	6
Yuengling Family	Brewers/1929	5
Schoedinger Family	Funeral and cremation services/1865	5
Zambelli Family	Fireworks/1893	4

FORTUNES LOST TOO SOON. WHAT WENT WRONG?

In addition to the Vanderbilts and the Robbies, the families in the following table also lost the family business and the money that accompanied it by the third generation—or earlier. In most cases, planning seemed to be almost nonexistent, and spending was rampant.

For example, published reports indicate that Huntington Hartford II, grandson of the founders and heir to the A & P fortune, invested heavily in businesses about which he had little understanding: art, movie production, the newspapers, and others. He also had several failed marriages that cost him millions of dollars, and his real estate holdings, including a home in London and an unsuccessful Paradise Island resort in the Bahamas, eventually drained the coffers. In general, it appears that those who lost their inheritances did so because they lived beyond their means for long periods of time.

Mark Twain lost it all while he was still alive, and most of his $10 million fortune disappeared because he had little business acumen and made a series of poor investment decisions.

Family	Business/Year Founded	Generations to Loss
Hartford Family	A&P Groceries/1859	3
Pulitzer Family	Communications/1878	3
Woolworth Family	Retailing/1879	3
Clemens Family (Mark Twain)	Author/Speaker	1

Notes

1. Steve Hargreaves, "Squandering the Family Fortune: Why Rich Families Are Losing Money," *CNN Money* (June 25, 2014), money.cnn.com/2014/06/25/luxury/family-wealth. Retrieved January 12, 2016.
2. Roy Williams and Vic Preisser, *Preparing Heirs: Five Steps to a Successful Transition of Family Wealth and Values* (Bandon, OR: Robert D. Reed Publishers, 2003), pp. 36–46.

CHAPTER 2

Wealth Is More Than Money

In the introduction to his transformational guidebook *Family Wealth: Keeping It in the Family*, James Hughes mentions that a family's wealth "consists primarily of its human capital (defined as all the individuals who make up the family) and its intellectual capital (defined as everything each individual family member knows), and secondarily of its financial capital."[1] Later in the book, he mentions a fourth type of capital: social capital, which I define as the networks of people of means who use their wealth and influence for the benefit of society.

If, in fact, human, intellectual, and social capital make up 75 percent of a family's actual wealth, giving 90 percent of the family's and advisors' attention to only 25 percent of the assets doesn't make a lot of sense. Yet this is the way traditional wealth managers and those they advise tend to view their roles.

Hughes makes exactly this point. In his view, a family that loses its wealth usually does so because of too great a concentration on financial capital and too little attention paid to the other types of capital the family possesses. Hughes goes on to say that "a family's financial capital is a tool to support the growth of the family's human and intellectual capital."[2] In other words, money is simply a means to a more important and meaningful end. Money, rightly considered, can empower an entire family, but if there is too much emphasis on balance sheets and not enough on family relationships, talents, roles, and strategic planning, the family can be enfeebled as its wealth trickles away.

Families who focus strictly on their financial assets usually do not sustain wealth over time and enjoy the fruits of their labor. They frequently have deep-rooted resentments about the uses of money, as well as relationship challenges, values clashes, and arguments about the place of money in their personal value systems. As a result, the wealth may disappear by the third generation, even if it is well-managed and invested.

11

The Rockefellers: An Emphasis on Wealth-Building and Philanthropy

If the Vanderbilt clan is the exemplar of wealth planning run amok, then the Rockefeller family is the other side of the coin. Although the Rockefellers no longer stand at the top of the heap of America's richest families, they still control more than $11 billion, settling in at #22 on the 2015 *Forbes* list of America's wealthiest families.

John D. Rockefeller, although probably no more ruthless than the other titans of his era—Vanderbilt, Carnegie, and Morgan, for example—could be savagely competitive, but buried within him was also a strand of philanthropy that grew as his assets expanded. An article in *Philanthropy Roundtable* highlights Rockefeller's charitable bent.

The article mentions that a few days after the sixteen-year-old Rockefeller landed his first job, he bought a ledger in which he accounted for virtually every cent of income and outgo. What is noticeable is that even when he was working for pennies each day, he already was sharing his resources. "'When I was only making a dollar a day,' Rockefeller later recalled, 'I was giving [away] five, ten, or twenty-five cents.'"[3]

As Rockefeller's wealth increased, so did his charitable donations. By 1865, he was giving away more than $1,000 annually. Not surprisingly, Rockefeller was inundated with requests for money. "At breakfast, he made it a habit to say grace and then open review of requests for charity . . . asking his children to further investigate promising appeals,"[4] thus setting the stage for their understanding of the need both for making money and making an impact; this understanding has continued into the succeeding generations.

Because of his immense fortune, Rockefeller's philanthropy, much of which was orchestrated and shepherded by his son, John D. Rockefeller Jr., was virtually boundless, from his founding of the University of Chicago to the Rockefeller Institute for Medical Research (now Rockefeller University) to the General Education Board to funding for Morehouse College and Spelman College (which was named for his wife, Laura Spelman Rockefeller). The contributions of the various organizations he funded are staggering to contemplate: a vaccine for yellow fever; prevention and cure of hookworm diseases; and support of sixty-four Nobel Prize winners in the fields of chemistry and medicine, to mention only a few. By the time of his death at age 97, Rockefeller had given away approximately $540 million and had changed countless lives forever.

In his adulthood, John D. Rockefeller Jr. also gave more than $500 million to conservation causes, historic preservation, art, and religious—primarily Baptist—institutions. He was the driving force behind New York's

Rockefeller Center. Through the establishment of the Rockefeller Brothers Fund (which also included their sister by 1954), the family continued the legacy of philanthropy, making grants to "organizations working to expand knowledge, clarify values and critical choices, nurture creative expression, and shape public policy."[5] Some of the trustees of the fund today are fourth and fifth generations of the Rockefeller family.

Not surprisingly, with the family's emphasis on public service, some of the third generation of Rockefellers found their way onto a larger stage—the political arena. Nelson Rockefeller served four terms as governor of New York and three years as vice president of the United States under Gerald Ford. His brother Winthrop was governor of Arkansas from 1967 to 1971.

In the minds of many, David Rockefeller was the embodiment of the Chase Manhattan Bank and later the Chase Manhattan Corporation. Beginning his affiliation with Chase Manhattan in 1946, he became chairman of the board of directors of Chase Manhattan Bank, NA, in March 1969 and CEO of Chase Manhattan Corporation in May of that year. He wielded immense influence in both corporate and international affairs.

Laurance Rockefeller carried on his father's work in conservation and was also an early venture capitalist. According to the *Washington Post*, "[he] also was a chief advocate for investing family money in new, often bold enterprises. Particularly fascinated by aviation, he poured money into new projects so they would not be snuffed out by a merger because of a lack of financing."[6] He was awarded the Presidential Medal of Freedom, the nation's highest civilian honor, for his unparalleled work in conservation.

John D. Rockefeller III, the eldest of the third generation, was active in the establishment of Lincoln Center in New York. He chaired the Rockefeller Foundation but used his own money to found the Population Council, an organization that dealt with world overpopulation issues; he later was appointed by President Richard Nixon to the Commission on Population Growth and the American Future. He was also an extensive collector of Asian art, which he bequeathed to the Asia Society, an organization he founded.

The only female among the third generation, Abigail (Babs) Rockefeller was a benefactor of note. The organizations that benefited from her philanthropy included Memorial Sloan-Kettering Cancer Center, the Metropolitan Museum of Art, the Museum of Modern Art (which was founded by her mother), the Population Council, the American Red Cross, and many more.

The fourth generation was represented in part by John D. "Jay" Rockefeller IV, son of John D. III. He was first elected governor of West Virginia in 1977, and in 1985 moved on to the U.S. Senate, where he served for thirty years.

In the nineteenth century, John D. Rockefeller amassed a fortune and became arguably the richest man in history. He saw around corners, seizing opportunities and acting aggressively in his own behalf, all the while giving away vast sums for the betterment of humankind. During that period, he was also the target of harsh criticism for some of his methods and actions, including monopolistic practices that were outlawed by the Sherman Antitrust Act. However, as the current head of the family, the centenarian David Rockefeller said, "Grandfather never breathed a sigh of remorse to my father, his grandchildren or anyone else. He believed Standard Oil benefited society."[7]

Thus, the Rockefeller slant on wealth certainly does not eschew continuing to acquire assets and to manage them for growth through Rockefeller & Co., which "serve[s] members of the Rockefeller family as they pursue their investment goals and further their heritage of public service and philanthropic endeavors."[8] However, the accumulation of wealth still is coupled with the family's agenda of "promoting the well-being of humanity around the world"[9] by making substantial grants to organizations that help the family realize their desire to do good. Today, a fifth generation of leaders is being groomed to take leadership of the family enterprise.

To cite only one example, in 2013, thirty-seven-year-old Justin Rockefeller, one of Jay Rockefeller's sons and a trustee of the Rockefeller Brothers Fund, co-founded (along with other social entrepreneurs and venture capitalists) The ImPact, a nonprofit NGO whose mission is "to inspire families to make more impact investments more effectively."[10]

The website of The ImPact lists several beliefs that John D. Rockefeller probably would have embraced. One can almost envision him nodding his head in agreement. Some of these beliefs include:

- *Big problems require bold action.*
- *We need to use all the tools in our belt to solve big problems.*
- *Profit and social impact are not mutually exclusive.*
- *Families can play a leading role.*[11]

Clearly, certain deeply held capitalistic principles and socially beneficial behaviors have been generationally transmitted. The family has attended not only to its financial capital but also to its intellectual, human, and social capital. The Rockefellers espouse a family philosophy of living well and doing good.

The Rockefellers can continue their outsize influence on the world by showing other wealthy families how to live well while also bringing about positive change. As Robert Frank said in a blog for the *Wall Street Journal*, "They are [...] an example of how rich families can stay together over multiple generations—largely through their family rituals and constant communication. . . . The Rockefellers may no longer be a force in business. But when it comes to unity and purpose, the name means as much as ever."[12]

Yes, the family has had its share of scandals and missteps, but in general, it has kept its eye on the ball. Family members know what matters to them as individuals and as a family, and they are a multigenerational success story.

The Rockefellers have chosen philanthropy as the way to act on their interests and passions. Other wealthy families may opt for avenues such as investing in new businesses, traveling the world, funding cutting-edge research in a disease that perhaps has affected a family member, or investing in groundbreaking technologies. The fact is that wealth is about the power of money or capital to bring about the results that matter to the wealth owner. Wealth is also about putting money in motion as a tool to create change.

All about Oprah

Take, for example, the only self-made African American woman billionaire in the United States: Oprah Winfrey. Although the talk show that made her a household name is no more, she continues to use her fortune to raise awareness about race in America and has produced a variety of African American–themed television programs and movies. She emphasizes the importance of education, especially of girls throughout the world, and she funds the Leadership Academy for Girls in South Africa. She is a tireless advocate for women and children's rights and has testified during congressional hearings on these topics. Her three foundations donate to such projects as the Charlize Theron Africa Outreach Project, Free the Children, Peace over Violence, Women for Women International, Women in the World Foundation, 46664 (Nelson Mandela's program that raises awareness of HIV/AIDS), and many others.

She also is involved in raising awareness of spirituality issues, regularly bringing thoughtful national and international spiritual leaders, writers, and artists—believers, atheists, and agnostics—to share points of view on the multiple award-winning *Super Soul Sunday* television program. Guests have ranged from the late Elie Wiesel and Wayne Dyer to Marianne Williamson and Thich Nhat Hanh, and millions of people have watched and listened to these programs.

Her wealth increases as her media empire expands, with ventures such as OWN (Oprah Winfrey Network) and *O* magazine—and through her own hard work. It is clear that her passion is for one thing: the empowerment of all people to help them live better lives, whether through education, spirituality, or some combination. She speaks little about money, but a great deal about the ability of people to raise themselves up, as she did, from whatever life circumstances claimed them at the beginning of their lives. That's where she puts her money, and that's where her heart seems to be. The Academy of Achievement, into which she was inducted in 1989, features her quote: "It doesn't matter who you are, where you come from. The ability to triumph begins with you. Always."

Finding a Singular Purpose

Maverick. Yachtsman. Founder of CNN and inventor of the 24-hour news cycle. Business mogul. Sports team owner. *Time* magazine's 1994 Man of the Year. Largest private landowner in the United States. They're all Ted Turner. With an independent streak and a fierce work ethic, Turner is a largely self-made success. Today, *Forbes* lists his fortune at approximately $2.2 billion, and Turner is using much of his wealth to foster the environmental causes in which he believes.

"I love this planet . . . I want to see the environment preserved and I want to see the human race preserved," he has said. "And I'd like to see everybody living decently in a more equitable, kind-hearted, thoughtful, generous world."[13] He has backed his philosophy with his treasure. By the mid-1990s, he owned approximately 1.7 million acres in Montana and began a project to reintroduce the Northern American bison to its native habitat by returning untold acres to their original natural state.

"It depends on what your area of interest is," he said in an interview for the March/April 2000 issue of *Philanthropy Roundtable*. "If you want to give to a university, they can use it in 20 years just as well. But if you care about the environment or population [his particular areas of concern], there are critical needs now."

That is not to say that Turner has not given to educational institutions. He has, and generously, but he concentrates now on challenges to the sustainability of the planet. He has found a mission and a passion and is using his wealth to support it.

Bill and Melinda Gates and Warren Buffett, among the richest of all the people in the world, originated the Giving Pledge, which is "an effort to help address society's most pressing problems by inviting the world's wealthiest individuals and families to commit to giving more than half of their wealth to philanthropy or charitable causes, either during their lifetime or in their will."[14] It is a moral commitment rather than a legal contract, and each individual or family who signs the pledge may designate where the money goes. Ted Turner is a signer, as are many household names who possess great wealth: David Rockefeller, Elon Musk, Richard Branson, Sara

Blakely, Mark Zuckerberg and Priscilla Chan, Barry Diller and Diane von Furstenberg—and more than 160 other individuals and families who may live a bit farther from the spotlight. The pledge, begun in the United States, now has signatories from other countries as well.

The Giving Pledge and The ImPact are sterling examples of Hughes's fourth component of wealth: social capital. Social capital is "the network of social connections that exists between people, and their shared values and norms of behavior, which enable and encourage mutually advantageous social cooperation."[15] Putting together people of like means increases their knowledge and understanding of the scope of the world's needs and encourages cooperation in solving thorny social problems through the application of wealth.

Certainly, all the people represented in The Giving Pledge continue to live richly, with perhaps only Buffett consciously choosing a more modest lifestyle. They continue to invest and increase their holdings. However, the majority of them also give away very large sums because they have found that wealth is not simply an accumulation of assets. They use those assets to make a difference in what matters to them.

The Advantages of Great Wealth ...

The effects of extensive holdings on individuals and families have been exhaustively studied, with results of various research projects sometimes seeming to contradict one another. In some ways, wealth appears to be an unalloyed good. It allows people to concentrate on their passions by offloading specialized tasks to family office personnel, household staff, and personal assistants. Wealth also makes it possible to seek the best society has to offer, often bypassing the traditional bureaucracy and processes that most other people have to endure.

The rich also have the means to pursue high-level experiential spending, and according to research published in the journal *Psychological Science*, experiential purchases, such as a family trip or an arts or educational endeavor, offer greater happiness than material purchases, such as houses, cars, planes, and expensive technology. "The anticipatory period [for experiential purchases] tends to be more pleasant ... less tinged with impatience relative to future material purchases we're planning on making," said Amir Kumar, one of the study's authors.[16]

Cornell University psychology professor Thomas Gilovich added, "People often make a rational calculation. [With limited money]... I can either go there, or I can have this. If I go there, it'll be great, but it'll be done in no time. If I buy this thing, at least I'll always have it. That is factually true, but not psychologically true."[17] This situation is called hedonic adaptation, and as soon as the novelty wears off a purchase, we are likely to be searching for the next one, which eventually we also will adapt to—and the cycle continues. Material goods, while often fun and pleasant to own, are not the road to happiness.

Ryan Howell, assistant professor of psychology at San Francisco State University, concurred with Gilovich. "What we find is that there's this huge misforecast," he says. "People think that experiences are only going to provide temporary happiness, but they actually provide both more happiness and more lasting value."[18]

Great wealth also makes great giving possible, and great giving produces happiness on both sides of the equation. Giving money away to people, institutions, and causes in which the donor believes has proven to be enjoyable, especially if the donor has a choice among options. Of course, it's also of great value to those who receive the gifts.

Elizabeth Dunn, who has conducted a variety of studies on the effects of giving money away, discovered that "while ... research has shown that people with more money are somewhat happier than people with less money, our research demonstrates that *how* people spend their money also matters for their happiness. . . . Both correlational and experimental studies show that people who spend money on others report greater happiness."[19]

... and the Drawbacks

Although great wealth can bring considerable happiness, it also can cause anxiety. In a major study titled "The Joys and Dilemmas of Wealth," conducted by the Boston College Center on Wealth and Philanthropy, the authors uncovered veins of discontent that often attend wealth.[20]

The 165 respondents to the survey had an average net worth of $78 million, with 120 exceeding $25 million. Among other concerns, the mega-rich who answered the survey mentioned that their biggest worry was their children's futures. If the children came into a large inheritance, they might become aimless, rudderless, and never find a satisfying career or other life purpose. However, if the parents left a huge legacy to charity instead, the children might be resentful and angry. With regard to inheritance, Warren Buffett has famously said, "A very rich person should leave his kids enough to do anything, but not enough to do nothing."

Additionally, if the children became wealthy in their own right, would they find mates who truly loved them or would they fall prey to fortune hunters? One respondent said poignantly, "I'm not super-rich. However, I do worry about affection; whether my wife married me ... for my money."

Some of the respondents noted that their friends believed the rich to be insulated from all concerns, not just financial problems. They mentioned that their friends sometimes discounted their griefs and worries because of the depth of their financial resources. As one wealthy interviewee put it, "When you are known to have money, people . . . act like you can buy your way out of any problem. They think you are impervious to . . . tragedy, sorrow or depression."

The wealthy are aware that some relationships are dependent on riches—that if people couldn't benefit financially from the friendship, they eventually would prove themselves to be false friends.

A surprising finding from the Boston College study was that the majority of respondents did not consider themselves to be financially secure and would require at least a quarter more than they currently had to achieve a feeling of security.

It's clear, then, that while wealth brings advantages, it's not all there is to living a rich life. If, as Hughes posits, money is an instrument families use to enhance their human and intellectual capital, and if wealth is aligned with a family's values, it may do much to cement relationships for generations. Concentration on money alone, however, can wreak havoc on family harmony. As one family member put it, "You really don't know your brothers and sisters until you share an inheritance with them. In our situation, it was pretty awful, even though I know my parents thought they had planned appropriately for all of us."

Helping individual family members and the family collective lead rich lives requires that financial capital serve as a catalyst to productivity and happiness. Under this definition of a rich life, if family members are happy and productive, and their wealth is aligned with their feelings of personal self-worth and an ongoing sense of fulfillment, they are likely to stay together and contribute to the sustainability and growth of the financial assets.

The Rich Life: A Case Study

A rich life can be visualized as a triangle, with each point representing an aspect of financial and personal success. When the triangle is too heavily weighted to one side, life is out of balance and can be unsatisfying, no matter the amount of money involved.

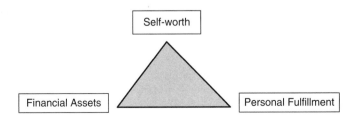

For example, Mark Allison* graduated from a prestigious Eastern business school and began a career in entrepreneurship. After building his business for fifteen years, he was successful, drawing a salary of about $300,000 per year. He employed 150 people, and his business continued to grow exponentially. Mark was excited to go to work every morning because he not only felt good about his personal success, but he also believed his accomplishments were useful and worthwhile, and he was proud of the business he continued to lead. He was happy to provide employment to talented people and to pay them well. He served on a few community boards he believed in, and he had a pleasant home life with his wife and three small children. His feelings of self-worth were high.

He also noted a sense of fulfillment because he was attaining goals he had set for himself and was driving toward even greater success. He worked fifty hours per week but he loved it because he was passionate about his vision for the future. He felt on track and that he was doing what he was called to do.

At this time, if Mark had been asked to graph the three factors of wealth, personal fulfillment, and self-worth, the resulting chart would likely have looked like this:

	Financial Assets	Sense of Self-Worth	Feelings of Fulfillment
5 (high)			
4			
3			
2			
1 (low)			

His graph shows all three factors in relative balance. Mark was reasonably financially successful, and his life also felt meaningful and rewarding.

After a few more years of business growth, Mark received an offer to buy his company for $250 million. He saw this offer as an opportunity to secure the future for himself and his family and to realize the rewards of his business accomplishments and success. If he continued to handle his money well, increasing his fortune through good management, he also could leave a legacy of wealth for future generations.

---

*The examples with an asterisk mentioned in this chapter are composites of cases the author has encountered in his wealth management career. Names and all identifying details have been changed to protect privacy.

Yet within six months Mark was in the midst of a gut-wrenching identity crisis. He had all the money he could ever need, but his business, which had been his chief reason to get up in the morning, was gone. His creativity shriveled and he was miserable. His wealth, sense of self-worth, and his purpose were no longer in alignment. He was not motivated. He felt guilty and anxious about the immense responsibility of managing his newfound wealth. Mark's reaction is far more common than people realize, because living a rich life is about more than money.

If he had been asked to draw his chart at that time, it would have reflected his out-of-balance life and his great unhappiness.

	Financial Accomplishment	Sense of Self-Worth	Feelings of Fulfillment
5 (high)			
4			
3			
2			
1 (low)			

After months of personal reflection, Mark engaged in a process that helped him understand his values, his strengths, and his passions. He was able to reconnect with what he loved about starting and building his business, and that discovery brought renewed joy to his life. Over time, Mark saw that a new way of living was possible. He could use his skills and drive for success to make a real difference in the lives of other talented entrepreneurs by investing in their companies and sharing his expertise with them. He could invest in the United States or in small companies in developing countries.

Although he did some investing in American firms, Mark found that his greatest happiness came from working in the developing world, where a relatively modest outlay could have amazing beneficial effects on villages and regions. He invested in schools, startup ventures, and infrastructure enhancements. Cooperating with local business leaders, he preserved cultural practices while also helping to raise the standard of living for everyone in the area. His sense of purpose was reignited, and he felt fulfilled as he achieved new goals and used his talents in novel and exciting ways. He took pleasure in his personal wealth and collaborated with his advisors to preserve and increase it, while at the same time using it in ways that made him happy. His previous success was now replicated on a much wider stage, and his new life was filled with zest and excitement.

His wife and children, who observed the reawakening of Mark's entrepreneurial genius, now have joined him in his gratifying pursuits. The children are comfortable in cultures throughout the world and look forward to continuing their father's work after they have completed their educations.

"If I had to draw my chart today," Mark says, "here's where I see myself. Providing my health holds out, I can imagine doing this for the rest of my life."

	Financial Accomplishment	Sense of Self-Worth	Feelings of Fulfillment
5 (high)			
4			
3			
2			
1 (low)			

Another View

In a 2015 graduation speech at the USC Marshall School of Business, Evan Spiegel, founder and CEO of Snapchat, explained why he turned down a $3 billion offer to buy the company, saying, "The fastest way to figure out if you are doing something truly important to you is to have someone offer you a bunch of money [for] it. If you sell, you . . . know . . . it wasn't the right dream . . . and if you don't sell . . . you're probably onto something."[21]

Spiegel created the company and obviously loves what he created. He also made a good business decision because between 2013, when he rejected the offer, and 2015, when he made the graduation speech, Snapchat's value had soared to approximately $15 billion, even though the company had yet to turn a profit. The valuation in mid-2016 was even higher, at approximately $20 billion. He has challenges to meet and apparently intends to stay the course, at least for the moment.[22] "There are very few people in the world who get to build a business like this," Spiegel said in an interview with *Forbes*. "I think trading that for some short-term gain isn't very interesting."[23] Apparently even if that short-term gain is in the billions.

Mark Allison's and Evan Spiegel's stories show that obsessing about money is to miss the point of life. Yes, to keep a fortune going throughout the generations, it's necessary to tend to and increase it so the assets are not diminished as the family grows through marriages and the addition of children. Equally important, however, is asking the hard strategic questions: What really matters to this family, and how will we make a difference, now and forever? What are our passions? What do we believe in, and how can we make our fortune serve those beliefs? Only a balanced combination of tactical and strategic planning adequately answers those questions and prepares the family for long-term influence and success.

Notes

1. James E. Hughes Jr., *Family Wealth: Keeping It in the Family* (New York: Bloomberg Press, 2004), p. xv.
2. Ibid., p. 17.
3. Philanthropy Roundtable, "The Rockefeller Legacy," www.philanthropyroundta ble.org/topic/excellence_in_philanthropy/the_rockefeller_legacy. Retrieved January 4, 2016.
4. Ibid.
5. Rockefeller Brothers Fund, www.rbf.org/grantees.
6. Adam Bernstein, "Laurance Rockefeller Dies at 94," *Washington Post* (July 12, 2004), www.washingtonpost.com/wp-dyn/articles/A43444-2004Jul11.html, Retrieved January 21, 2016.
7. Abram Brown, "25 Lessons from 100-Year-Old David Rockefeller, The World's Oldest Billionaire, *Forbes* (June 12, 2015), www.forbes.com/sites/abrambrown/ 2015/06/12/25-life-lessons-from-100-year-old-david-rockefeller-the-worlds-oldest-billionaire. Retrieved January 4, 2016.
8. Rockefeller & Co., www.rockco.com/our-history. Retrieved January 4, 2016.
9. The Rockefeller Fund, www.rockefellerfoundation.org/. Retrieved January 4, 2016.
10. The ImPact, theimpact.org/#the-pact.
11. Ibid.
12. Robert Frank, blogs.wsj.com/wealth/2008/05/27/do-the-rockefellers-still-matter, May 27, 2008. Retrieved January 4, 2016.
13. www.brainyquote.com/quotes/authors/t/ted_turner.html. Retrieved January 21, 2016.
14. The Giving Pledge, givingpledge.org.
15. "Social Capital," dictionary.reference.com/browse/social-capital.
16. www.psychologicalscience.org/index.php/news/releases/anticipating-experience-based-purchases-more-enjoyable-than-material-ones.html.
17. Andrew Blackman, "Can Money Buy You Happiness?" *Wall Street Journal* (November 10, 2014), www.wsj.com/articles/can-money-buy-happiness-heres-what-science-has-to-say-1415569538. Retrieved January 11, 2016.
18. Ibid.
19. Elizabeth Dunn, Lara Aknin, and Michael Norton, "Spending Money on Others Promotes Happiness," greatergood.berkeley.edu/ . . . /norton-spendingmoney. pdf. Retrieved January 12, 2016.

20. Gerald Le Van, "Wealth: Its Joys and Its Discontents: The Boston College Study," Upchurch, Watson, White, and Max (April 2011), www.uww-adr.com/blog/wealth-its-joys-and-its-discontents-the-boston-college-survey. Retrieved January 16, 2016.

21. Evan Spiegel, "Snapchat CEO Evan Spiegel to Grads: 'This Is the World We Were Born Into, and We Are Responsible for It,'" *Time* (May 16, 2015), time.com/3881609/snapchat-evan-spiegel-graduation-speech. Retrieved October 4, 2016.

22. Andrew Nusca, "Why Snapchat Is Worth $19 Billion (or More)," Fortune (February 19, 2015), fortune.com/2015/02/19/snapchat-worth-19-billion-more, retrieved January 13, 2016.

23. J. J. Colao, "The Inside Story of Snapchat: The World's Hottest App or a $3 Billion Disappearing Act?" *Forbes* (January 6, 2013), www.forbes.com/sites/jjcolao/2014/01/06/the-inside-story-of-snapchat-the-worlds-hottest-app-or-a-3-billion-disappearing-act/3/#2715e4857a0bb4e75f542d41. Retrieved January 13, 2016.

CHAPTER 3

The Impact of Wealth Stewardship

The concept of stewardship is thousands of years old. In medieval times, domestic stewards oversaw the finances and activities of the household while village stewards represented the lord in towns over which the lord had jurisdiction. It was critical that a steward be honest and trustworthy and to act in his lord's best interest.

More recently, stewardship has taken on a broader meaning and is now defined as "the ... responsible management of something entrusted to one's care."[1] A steward may be a teacher entrusted with educating children or an elected official charged with managing a municipality. In the realm of wealth management, serving as a trustee for a family trust exemplifies the concept of stewardship of a different type. Essentially, anyone assigned to caring for and making decisions in the best interests of something or someone outside him- or herself is a steward.

Many wealth creators or inheritors of substantial resources come to a point at which they recognize that their wealth is more than they will need or ever spend, and it has the potential to last far beyond their lifetimes. When they arrive at this realization, they may begin to feel and understand the weight of their responsibility and the magnitude of their opportunity as wealth stewards. For these families, wealth can be like a big rock thrown into a pond. The ripple effect the rock creates has the potential to be either positive or negative. Every decision (or non-decision) comes with implications that can have an impact on every member of the family and other potential constituents of the wealth. Some people choose to embrace their circumstances and others consciously or subconsciously avoid addressing them.

In their book, *Family Legacy and Leadership: Preserving True Family Wealth in Challenging Times*,[2] Mark Haynes Daniell and Sarah S. Hamilton point out two attitudes that are prevalent with regard to family wealth. Some view themselves as inheritors or *proprietors,* with little or no desire to administer or preserve their assets for future generations. Instead, they are consumers of wealth who use their assets primarily for their own well-being and to support only current family members or others who are present in their lives at the moment. The second group, in contrast, has a far greater sense of themselves as *"stewards,"* feeling a strong obligation to manage and sustain the wealth for their current family, their future family members, and important societal causes that have meaning to them. Those who identify as stewards are more likely to work together as a family group while proprietors tend go it alone and are more insular in their decision making.

Both proprietors and stewards usually engage in good tactical financial and estate planning to manage their fortunes prudently, reduce their tax burdens, provide for efficient asset distribution, and create vehicles to manage wealth on behalf of family members and other causes that are important to them. All of these activities are critical, but effective wealth management and stewardship involve much more: understanding the purpose and benefits of shared ownership; identifying individual and shared family values; developing a family mission statement and decision-making process; identifying and clarifying roles; cultivating future leaders; providing ongoing, generationally specific wealth education for family members; and creating a plan for consistent and cohesive communication.

A stewardship model of multigenerational wealth management harnesses the family's energy, creativity, and capacity to continue shaping the future for themselves, the communities in which they live, and the greater good of the world if they so choose. Effective stewardship enables the family to do the following:

- Leverage all the collective capacity and resources of the family, including its financial, human, intellectual, and social capital.
- Empower each generation to focus on sustaining their collective resources rather than dissipating them.
- Maintain clarity and understanding regarding the roles and responsibilities of family members as current and future owners.
- Develop a leadership model the family understands and supports and that allows for effective and efficient decision making.
- Provide a well-defined family communication structure that ensures all family members are kept abreast of the information necessary to maintain their trust and support.
- Sustain the family's wealth, well-being, and continuity for generations and allow them the potential to put their thumbprint on history for a protracted period of time.

Proprietors, on the other hand, may take conscious or unintended actions that severely curtail the ability to preserve wealth or sustain the family's shared resources, such as the following:

- Focus only on tactical financial, tax, and estate planning issues without considering the implications those decisions will have on family members and their relationships.
- Maintain a high level of control both during their lifetimes and after death through the use of restrictive and complex legal structures.
- Avoid sharing information and keep important details confidential.
- Neglect to remember, articulate, and enact the family's core values, mission, expectations, and roles in managing the wealth.

This is not to say that families must either preserve or spend their money; a carefully developed strategic wealth management plan allows for both living well and doing good. Ideally, planning should begin while the wealth creator is still available and continue throughout the succeeding generations.

Three Families: The Hands-on Patriarch

Raymond Bergmond* grew up in Green Bay, Wisconsin. He was born in 1948 to enterprising parents who were children of the Great Depression. Ray was raised with traditional American values: hard work, perseverance, self-reliance, and individual independence. His parents owned two small grocery stores and encouraged Ray and his siblings to strive for more. While still a young teenager, Ray came home from school every day to work at the meat counter in one of his parents' stores. During his high school years, there was little time for much more than going to school, laboring at the family business, and completing his homework. It was not an easy life, but it was better than many, and it was the one he knew.

After high school, Ray worked his way through the University of Wisconsin. Upon graduation, he landed a sales job at a large manufacturing company, advancing to sales manager in only two years. He worked hard and found satisfaction in his job, but he was restless and wanted more. He decided that rather than work his whole life for someone else, he would become an entrepreneur and chase the American dream. Using a small loan from his father and another from an uncle, Ray established his fledging business. He named it Bergmond

---

*The examples with an asterisk mentioned in this chapter are composites of cases the author has encountered in his wealth management career. Names and all identifying details have been changed to protect privacy.

Custom Glass and could not have been more proud the first day he was open for business.

After nearly forty years of blood, toil, tears, and sweat, Ray was CEO of BCG Manufacturing, a multimillion-dollar closely held business in which he and his wife, Sara, were the only stockholders. Ray and Sara had three children Ray barely knew. His eldest son, Joe,* the thirty-four-year-old divorced father of Melissa and Raymond II, worked in the family business as vice president of sales and marketing. Ray's younger son, Robert,* was a naval officer often based thousands of miles from home. He and his wife had two pre-adolescent boys. The third sibling, Jennifer,* married with three young daughters, was a homemaker focused on raising her children. Her husband, Kyle,* worked in the family business as a sales manager reporting to Joe. Robert and Jennifer always had been made to feel somewhat less important or worthy because they did not want to be part of their father's enterprise and be ruled by his rigid standards and heavy hand.

Ray was a my-way-or-the-highway martinet who had expected all of his children to enter the family business. However, he gave them scant information about the company, and the oldest, Joe, who followed in Dad's footsteps, did so only because that decision had been his father's destiny for him from the day Joe was born.

Once he was part of the corporation, Joe understood that the family was far richer than he had thought, but his father was still closed-mouthed about his personal wealth. Kyle later joined the company after Ray insisted he build a successful career and support Jennifer and the family in the way Ray deemed appropriate.

When their children were young, Ray and Sara lived a comfortable middle-class lifestyle, but well below their means because they did not believe in conspicuous consumption and did not want to encourage friendships they perceived to be based on their wealth. In addition, they never shared anything about their resources or wealth planning with the next generation, believing if they did so they would sap their children's initiative and drive. Not wanting the kids to be spoiled, entitled brats, Ray guarded all his company and personal financial information, barely sharing it even with Sara. The children did not know his attorney or his financial advisors.

Several years into his tenure in the family enterprise, Joe's relationship with his father became strained because Ray ruled his company with an iron fist. Joe wanted to test new ideas, new technologies, and new markets, but Ray always resisted. "My leadership and management have been successful in growing this company for forty years," Ray often told Sara. "I don't need suggestions or advice from someone who's been in my business for just a few years. Joey's still young and inexperienced. He needs to learn from me, not from all the professors at that fancy business school. An MBA is nice, but it's not a substitute for hands-on experience."

What Ray didn't realize was that his intransigent attitude and reluctance to share power deprived Joe of the very experience his father valued—and made it more likely that Joe would make mistakes when he took over the business.

A few months shy of his sixty-ninth birthday, while working late in his office as he normally did, Ray had a fatal heart attack. Sara and the family were shocked at his abrupt passing but not surprised he died at his desk. They had all expected him to go exactly that way. Now they had to manage the future without his guidance, and neither Sara nor the children had any idea about his financial planning. Ray had managed all of their business and personal financial matters. Sara had gone to their attorney and signed documents as she was told to do, but she never really understood them. Ray always let her know that everything was taken care of, and she loved and trusted him. She knew he had built a fantastic business, so she believed he also must have done a fine job of managing the family's wealth for the future.

Ray had spent time with his attorney and accountant structuring his and Sara's estates in the way he believed was best for his family. Nonetheless, at the reading of his will, Robert and Jennifer, who were unaware of the extent of their father's wealth, were stunned by the value of the assets their father had accumulated. It had the potential to be life-changing for all of them. At the same time, however, they discovered that the wealth was tied up in restrictive legal structures.

All the stock in BCG Manufacturing was transferred to a trust with Sara as the current income beneficiary and the three children as the remaindermen in equal shares. Joe, Sara, and Ray's attorney, John Melvin,* were appointed as co-trustees. A separate trust was then set up for Sara with financial assets to support her lifestyle. Joe was appointed as trustee of this trust and trustee of two other trusts set up for his brother and sister.

Robert and Jennifer were appalled to discover the trusts were so limiting—and that they had to ask Joe for any distributions from their trusts. Ray never had discussed this strategy with his children, so even Joe was surprised and unprepared for this new role. He had no clue what was required to be a trustee. He also wondered why his father had chosen him for this overwhelming responsibility, and since he was familiar only with autocratic management, he applied it to both his father's company and his dealings with his newly dependent brother and sister. Robert and Jennifer expressed their anger and resentment to Sara, who felt stuck in the middle and only wanted everyone to get along. She was lonely after Ray's death, and it disturbed her that her children were tense with each other and with her.

The two younger siblings were embittered by the way their brother wielded his authority. "My father left me that money," Jennifer said. "Why should I have to jump through Joe's hoops to receive something that's rightfully mine?"

"Dad's trying to rule us from the grave through Joe," Robert added. "Why did he give Joe veto power over something I might want to do for my own family? I should be grieving my dad, and instead I'm mad at him. I'm mad at my brother, too, because I have to go to him hat in hand for something Dad left for me and my family. He's as tough as Dad, and I have to justify everything to get a penny. I've dealt with tough captains and admirals, but they don't hold a candle to Joe."

Jennifer and Robert formed an alliance against their brother's trusteeship, hiring lawyers to try to break the trusts and free up the funds. After a long battle, Joe resigned as trustee because he was overwhelmed with running the company and dealing with his family.

In the midst of the legal actions, Joe struggled to keep his father's business running smoothly. Kyle ultimately left BCG due to the fractured relationship between his wife and her brother. Joe was working sixty hours a week trying to replace his father and maintain the company. After a period of adjustment and several costly missteps, he was angry, tired, and overwhelmed. He realized he needed to sell the company to keep it from being destroyed from within. Ultimately, he sold to Standard Glass Company for a low valuation because a quick sale was required to retain the remaining customers.

Due to the legal battles and the forced sale of the company, Ray's family is still at odds. Sara spends her time with her grandchildren, trying to be the glue that holds the Bergmond family together. With her coaxing, the children are trying to repair their relationship, but it is slow going because their trust in each other has been damaged, perhaps irreparably.

Ray's business was absorbed by Standard and the legacy of its name, which was so important to Ray, is gone forever. Joe is still recovering from the trauma of selling the company and trying to find meaning in his life. In the meantime, though there will be sufficient money for this generation of Ray's family, it's a toss-up as to whether the seven grandchildren will profit from Ray's entrepreneurial success.

Three Families: The Silver Spoon

Patterson (Pat) Kaufman's* grandfather Jacob* amassed a fortune in real estate development throughout the United States. His son, Charles,* Pat's father, was prepared from adolescence to take over Kaufman Properties,* becoming a vice president at twenty-five, senior vice president at twenty-nine, and executive vice president at thirty-one. Upon his father's retirement, Charles became president and CEO at the age of forty-six. An able leader and businessman, Charles increased the value of the company stock and took a hefty and well-deserved salary for his exceptional stewardship of the asset his father had entrusted to him. At fifty, his net worth was more than $200 million.

As they grew up, it would have been hard for Pat and his sister, Meghan,* not to have known they were extremely wealthy. Their home was among the largest in Atlanta, employing a house manager, cook, housekeeper, and gardener. Their mother, Lydia,* was known for her lavish parties and involvement in several charities. The children attended the best private schools and were showered with money, cars, travel, and expensive gifts for holidays and birthdays. The only financial lessons they received from their parents, however, were warnings about scam artists and charlatans. As a result, it was hard for them to build trusting relationships as they grew up. Although eventually things turned out well for both children, they experienced some bumps in the road due to the confusing dynamics money created in their lives.

Pat often was embarrassed by his family's wealth and felt isolated. Because buildings had neither perceptions nor opinions, he discovered a passion for architecture and historic preservation when he was still in high school. Following his graduation from Cornell, he chose to attend the Columbia Graduate School of Architecture, Planning, and Preservation.

Although he did not yet have a lot of practical experience, Pat convinced Charles he would be a valuable asset to the firm—and that new development didn't always mean new buildings. Once Charles felt that Pat had paid his dues, he gave his son the opportunity to develop a project outside Nashville, Tennessee. Using his intelligence and passion, Pat saved the area from the company's wrecking ball by transforming a collection of decrepit industrial buildings into a vibrant, walkable community with a farmers' market, local shops and restaurants, a centrally located park and playground, and affordable houses that were perfect for Millennials who chose not to make long commutes from the suburbs. The old eyesore became the place for young people to live, work, shop, eat, and enjoy life.

Although the new neighborhood was a company project, Pat also financed part of it with his own money, which he had received at the end of his graduate education. He continued to underwrite improvements that were important to his concept, eventually persuading his father to add a portfolio of preservation ventures to the company's development efforts.

As time passed, Charles groomed Pat to become president and CEO of the company at the age of forty. However, at about the same time, a well-known nonprofit preservation foundation became aware of Pat's efforts in the South and asked him to become its executive director. Taking that opportunity would require Pat to relocate to Chicago, and the salary was smaller than he would make with his father. Nonetheless, the job aligned perfectly with Pat's interests and passion. Pat was independently wealthy and could live well even if he didn't earn the huge salary, stock, and bonuses his father promised. The new job was his dream and he felt he was born to do it, even if his father thought differently.

Enamored by the opportunity to make a difference doing work he loved, Pat took the job. His heartbroken father disowned him, citing his son's disloyalty to the family business and legacy. Shortly thereafter, with Pat gone and Meghan unprepared to take over, Charles sold Kaufman Properties to Seaver Development* and retired at the age of sixty-eight.

"What Dad didn't understand," Pat said, "was that he had implanted in me a very strong concept of stewardship. He took my grandfather's business further than his father could ever have imagined. He employed hundreds of people. He kept the business together during hard times. I learned from him. It's just that my stewardship took a different direction. I prefer to be the steward of the country's architectural and historic heritage. My dad and I are more alike than he thought, but he couldn't see it."

Meghan's story was different. When she was a senior in college, she listened to her sorority sisters' plans for postgraduate education and jobs, but realized she had no interest in or need to consider those options and now had little in common with her friends.

Meghan also was struggling with the fact that she would inherit several million dollars on the day of commencement. The responsibility was overwhelming to her. She became more and more anxious as her graduation approached. "What had I ever done to have so much when many others have so little? It didn't make sense to me."

Following her college years, Meghan was adrift and had difficulty finding herself. After graduation, she bought a luxury penthouse, a new wardrobe, and an expensive car, but she didn't know what else to do with her money—or her life. She was asked to serve on a few charitable boards, but soon figured out that in nearly every case her invitation was based on whether she was willing to make large contributions to the charities. She remembered her parents' earlier cautions about people who might take advantage of her. Feeling personally devalued and used, she resigned from each organization shortly after she joined.

Meghan became distrustful and had difficulty forming relationships, especially with men. She broke off her engagement when it seemed to her that her fiancé showed much more interest in her money than he did in her. Her social life was nearly nonexistent because she had almost nothing to share with other women her age. Her wealth both insulated and isolated her. She was lonely and felt she could trust no one but her brother.

Lost and bewildered, Meghan finally happened upon an organization that intrigued her: a small foundation that provided shelter for homeless women and children. She dug in and discovered that homeless children usually didn't go to school because they moved so often, from shelter to shelter or living for a brief time with relatives or friends before moving on again. Their nomadic existence meant that even the brightest children typically were far behind their chronological peers in school.

Meghan saw this organization as a chance to use her wealth in a way that could produce concrete results for people who had so much less than she. Finally, and maybe for the first time in her life, she found true satisfaction in using her wealth to do something that had meaning for her. Meeting like-minded people, she enjoyed an uptick in her social life and found she didn't need to be suspicious of her new friends.

Using the clout her name and inheritance provided, Meghan conferred with the governmental group that oversaw all community shelters in the area. She then worked with local school officials and others to develop a comprehensive education plan for homeless children. It included online options, certified teachers and classrooms within the shelters, enrichment activities such as trips to local science centers and museums, extensive libraries, and more. Although the project received some grants for materials, Meghan self-funded the addition of classroom trailers at three shelters, transportation to outside educational venues, and the purchase of a wonderful selection of volumes for the libraries. She paid for the technology improvements required for online classes and for all of the texts and workbooks. She was working more than fifty hours a week and enjoying every second of it.

As she felt more and more empowered by the wealth that had once threatened to engulf her, Meghan also began to support similar initiatives for women. They, too, were provided with educational opportunities and vocational training so they could leave the streets and shelters and live independently. "It was by far the most rewarding thing I could have done with my money," she said. "It was fortunate I wasn't expected to go into the family business, and my parents were proud of what I was doing. It broke my heart that they couldn't see the value of Pat's contributions once he left the company."

Once Meghan had found her place, she became far more interested in the stewardship of her fortune, investing in the future of children, and working to end homelessness. She turned to her father's advisors to learn how to sustain the money and increase her assets while carrying out the work that had become so important to her. After her father sold his company, she also sought his advice, bringing him an idea for affordable housing that would allow women and children to rent a modest home and get back on their feet.

Charles was enthusiastic about the concept, helping Meghan navigate the politics, procedures, and permissions required for her small housing development. Meghan, like her brother, used her private wealth to accomplish the project, paying for the construction of ten small houses.

Children of immense privilege, Pat and Meghan saw the family fortune as a means to accomplish great things, not as an end in itself. Although the breach between father and son still is not fully repaired, they are trying to understand one another. Neither Pat nor Meghan has married yet. Even if they do, what they have learned from their own experiences has convinced them that a large portion of their wealth will support charities and organizations that will carry on their personal legacies of community stewardship.

Three Families: The Middle Ground

Like Ray, Alicia McMillian,* born in 1955, lived in the Midwest. Alicia's mother was a secretary and her dad owned an auto body shop. Although the family was not impoverished, money was always tight. Alicia's parents budgeted carefully and made every dollar count. She followed their examples of both industry and thrift. These lessons would serve her well in the future.

During her teen years, Alicia worked summers as a service writer in her father's shop, saving her salary to go to college. Eventually, she took over the bookkeeping and banking for her father's business. Well-liked by customers for her charming personality, she also was exceptionally bright and graduated as valedictorian of her high school class.

Due to her intelligence and hard work in high school, Alicia was accepted by several of the best universities in the country. She had a strong sense of adventure, so she decided to head across the country to attend Stanford University. While at Stanford, she studied hard, did well, and built a terrific business network through her aggressive pursuit of internships and special programs that introduced her to well-known executives.

After graduation, she joined Crestrock Partners,* a venture capital firm in Palo Alto that focused on investing in early-stage technology startups. With clients including the biggest names in the high-tech industry, the partners jumped into the ultra-high-net-worth category in short order. After about ten years, Alicia was named managing partner of the firm.

During her term as a partner for Crestrock, Alicia met and eventually married Matthew Farcus,* a lawyer who handled initial public offerings and mergers and acquisitions. Three years after their marriage, Alicia and Matthew became parents to twin girls, Gwen* and Stephanie.* For the first few years after the girls were born, Alicia continued working, tending to her growing family with the help of a nanny and a housekeeper. As the family's wealth grew from the success of Crestrock, she cut back on her constant involvement with the business, promoting trusted associates into positions of authority as she strove for some life balance. She remained managing partner and the face of the company, but left much of the daily operations to other members of the Crestrock team.

After long conversations with her husband, Alicia decided that she would leave Crestrock to pursue other interests, such as her family, proactive management of the family's wealth, entrepreneurship, and philanthropy. As a part of her new focus, Alicia decided to return some of her good fortune to the community that had made her a multimillionaire by making impact investments that would create a financial as well as a social return. Together with Matthew, she established the McMillian Farcus Family Investment Partnership, an investment holding company that provided seed capital for innovative ideas generated by female entrepreneurs.

Alicia and Matt talked a great deal about their hopes and concerns regarding their daughters and the effect their wealth could have on them. Being in the venture capital and legal worlds, they had seen how wealth could destroy a family if not handled carefully. With this in mind, they sought advice on how to manage both the strategic and tactical issues of wealth management, so both the assets and the family would grow in positive ways.

They hired Willson & Moyers Wealth Management Advisors* to help them lay out and implement a plan for long-term wealth stewardship. James Moyers* worked with them to develop a program that included semiannual family meetings, a defined wealth education program for the girls, and an investment model based on the specific purposes for their wealth.

When their daughters were old enough, Alicia and Matt invited Gwen and Stephanie to family meetings. They always had included the girls in informal dinner table conversations about the family's future, but now the daughters were an important part of the meetings with the wealth advisory group. During these family meetings, Alicia and Matt shared current projects for the girls' input, allowing them to read and make comments on the funding proposals submitted to the company. Gwen and Stephanie were as involved as they wanted to be, and their parents paid attention to their ideas and their feedback.

The girls asked lots of questions and learned a great deal over the years. They had a voice but no vote until they were of legal age; by the time they became voting members of the board, they were conversant with the qualities of good proposals and how new businesses were sustained. They were kept abreast of the investments and the results of investment decisions. They also gained an understanding and an opportunity to provide input on the vision for the McMillian Farcus Family Investment Partnership.

During these meetings with James and other advisors, Matt and Alicia made sure their daughters understood the nature of the inheritance they would someday receive. The discussions were age-appropriate and included not only information about money, but also about the family's values. Both girls understood from an early age that their parents would leave them a relatively small amount of direct wealth. Instead, they planned to distribute the majority of their assets to a family foundation of which Gwen and Stephanie would serve as board members.

Alicia always had found satisfaction in her work of investing in growing companies, but she didn't pressure her daughters to go into the business. Nonetheless, their college experiences led them into fields that dovetailed with their mother's interests. Gwen majored in business at her mother's alma mater. Stephanie was intrigued with helping women from developing countries improve their lives, so after college she traveled to India with Women's Centers International. During her time in Mumbai, she worked in projects designed to improve the status of women. She loved the experience, but after two years she became homesick and returned to the United States.

When Stephanie was in India, she was not surprised to find wide gaps in the quality of healthcare among different population groups, but she was shocked—and horrified—to discover the disparities in healthcare for women and children in her own home state. She spoke at length with Gwen, and the two decided they wanted to build something important with their parents.

Combining their strengths and armed with their intimate knowledge of how projects receive funding, the sisters wrote a proposal and approached their parents to become investors in their new business—one which focused on the use of technology to improve access to healthcare in minority communities. Their original proposal was to carry out an extensive pilot project that involved connecting homes, church clinics, and a network of physician offices to identify and deal with health problems in a nascent stage, thereby improving the well-being of the community and saving healthcare dollars.

Rather than being disappointed that neither child was interested in taking the helm at McMillian Farcus Family Investment Partnership, Alicia and Matt reviewed the girls' plans and eagerly became part of their team. "I invest in young women's businesses all the time. Why wouldn't I become an investor in my own daughters' idea? They're well-schooled, bright, and prepared. I'm proud that they didn't simply ask Matt and me for a handout, but approached the entire project with professionalism. I'm sure their new venture will be successful and perhaps become a model for the entire country. I see a true entrepreneurial spark in this important work. It's inventive, creative, and fills a vital need. I'm happy to serve as an advisor to the project."

Now both in their sixties, Alicia and Matt are preparing to fund the foundation their daughters will take over at the appropriate time. The couple plans to travel widely and perhaps live abroad for a while. They hope their daughters will make happy marriages, because Matt and Alicia eagerly await grandchildren.

The three families in these examples have taken different approaches to the stewardship of money, and each shows that the direction of the second generation is largely determined by the actions of the first. Discussion is critical. Values around the use of money cannot be shared if the conversations are never held. Unspoken expectations can sully the family's relationships with one another while lack of preparation can result in painful consequences that last for decades.

First-generation wealth creators who dictate the path their heirs are expected to follow and do not prepare them for the responsibilities, pleasures, and pitfalls of wealth run the risk that succeeding generations will feel like tenants in their own lives. However, careful preparation, education, and communication create both an ownership mentality and a growth mindset. Heirs come to understand that the family is not the name on the building, but is instead a living organism, a supportive network, and a catalyst for stability and continued progress.

Notes

1. *Merriam-Webster's Collegiate Dictionary Eleventh Edition.*
2. Mark Haynes Daniell and Sarah S. Hamilton, *Family Legacy and Leadership: Preserving True Family Wealth in Challenging Times* (Asia: John Wiley & Sons, 2010), pp. 19–20.

PART II

Understanding the Wealth Management Process

CHAPTER 4

The Importance of Integrating Tactical and Strategic Wealth Management

As currently structured, the wealth management industry provides tactical wealth management services to the clients it serves. Families of significant resources often employ wealth management teams comprising some combination of attorneys for estate planning, entity formation, and tax planning; accountants for recordkeeping, tax planning, and tax compliance; financial planners for cash flow, investment management, tax planning, and insurance; investment managers for portfolio management, asset allocation, security selection, and performance reporting; insurance agents/brokers for life, health, property, and casualty insurance planning and product selection; and bankers for advice on banking, lending, and deposits.

Law firms, accounting firms, registered investment advisors, banks, and insurance companies that provide wealth management and wealth preservation services for well-to-do clients spend 90 to 95 percent of their resources on the tactical products and solutions mentioned in the previous paragraph.

These services are indispensable for helping families manage and sustain their resources. However, the professionals who staff these firms generally have little understanding or expertise in dealing with the strategic challenges that can arise when attempting to serve an ultra-high-net-worth family made up of multiple units and often including three, four, or five generations. The families may have multiple legal entities; passive investments and operating businesses; and competing and contrasting interests, viewpoints, and opinions. It's possible they don't agree on such issues as how to use the resources of the family, how to determine the role each family member should play, how to communicate effectively among various family groups, and how the family enterprise should be managed—and while traditional wealth managers have expertise in overseeing and transferring the assets, the intricacies of family relationships, family organizational styles, structures, responsibilities, and communication mechanisms are generally beyond their scope and training.

In addition, the fee and compensation models of traditional wealth managers focus on tactical planning and performance in the short run, not strategic planning to support family continuity and long-term wealth sustainability.

When wealth owners realize that they need help with strategic planning as well as tactical execution, they may investigate firms that offer the consulting services traditional wealth management neglects: identifying independent and shared family values, mission, and vision planning; role definition and clarification; leadership growth and family wealth education; communication planning; and family governance, to name a few.

These specialized firms often are staffed with experts whose backgrounds are in psychology, leadership development, or business and management consulting. Although they provide valuable and much-needed services to the families they work with, these people normally do not have a strong understanding of the tactical issues and solutions required by ultra-high-net-worth families.

These two service models exist at opposite ends of the wealth management spectrum. Standing alone, they deliver incomplete and fragmented service to the families who call upon them for assistance and support.

The lack of integration puts the responsibility on the families to align their strategic and tactical planning and avoid the "shirtsleeves to shirtsleeves" phenomenon. Families must integrate both strategic and tactical planning to ensure effective management of the current resources, continued wealth creation, long-term sustainability, continuity, and family harmony as they navigate the myriad issues of shared wealth. The family may not have the capacity to manage both halves of the equation, or indeed, either one.

Ultra-high-net-worth families often don't begin to think deeply about wealth management until they experience a liquidity event or another transitional situation such as the retirement or death of a significant family owner. Suddenly, the family is either dealing with an inflow of cash or a requirement to raise cash—perhaps multiple millions of dollars—and family members are forced to address the present situation and to think about the future: How do they protect what they have and make it grow, both to benefit their families and to create the legacy they want to leave? Often surprised and overwhelmed by the host of opportunities and risks they are facing, they review their current advisory team and perhaps add new advisors.

They may choose this somewhat inchoate group of advisors based on the recommendations of friends or other advisors. They also might conduct a somewhat random research process and end up handing over important aspects of their lives to relative strangers.

As Rogers, Budge, and Lambergs mentioned, "Family decision-making processes are sometimes not only opaque to advisors, but also aren't clear among family members themselves."[1]

Without a well-articulated process for making decisions about advisors, "families end up frustrated by meeting a large number of advisory organizations ... and ... floundering due to an inability to respond to the volume of polarized views and conflicts that arise."[2]

Close questioning of potential advisors is vital because ultra-high-net-worth families have special needs and often bring a large number of family members and considerable complexity to the table.

The Beginning: Questions and Answers about Strategic and Tactical Wealth Planning

Families who want to work with firms that (1) provide an integrated approach to wealth management and (2) have a deep understanding of the unique strategic and tactical issues that accompany significant shared wealth should ask the following questions:

- *How many clients do you have that fit our profile with regard to net worth, family composition, business enterprise, and particular needs?* If the firm predominately manages affluent clients with only a few who are truly ultra-high-net-worth, the advisory team may not have sufficient understanding of the unique issues and intricacies of a family group with at least $30 million in investable assets, which is the benchmark that Investopedia uses to define this group of individuals and families.[3] Credit Suisse sets the benchmark at $50 million, but whatever the definition, those who fall into this category are a distinctive group of clients with unique needs.
- *How many clients does your firm, advisor, or team manage in total?* If it's hundreds of families, the ultra-high-net-worth family may not receive the attention required to manage the multiple details that go into making important decisions.
- *What is the client-to–team member ratio?* How many teams are designated to ultra-high-net-worth families? Because of the formidable nature of these families' needs, the ratio should be small enough to serve them effectively. Depending on the team or advisor structure, one senior relationship manager can comfortably manage about six to ten clients. An advisory team can effectively support roughly twenty families, but probably not more.

- *What is the composition of the team servicing our relationship?* What are the educational backgrounds, business and professional experiences, and tenure of the practitioners working with the family? To effectively serve the family on both a strategic and tactical level, the group of advisors must have backgrounds in law, accounting, investment management, tax planning, risk management, and organizational management. In addition, how long have the team members been working with their current firms? Continuity and consistency of the advisors is important, so the team knows the family as it evolves. A revolving door of new advisors who must be constantly retrained about the family's circumstances and objectives is of little use.

  Not all the team members have to be with one company. In fact, since several different disciplines are necessary, it's likely the advisors will come from several firms. For example, only practicing attorneys may give legal advice and draft legal documents. Therefore, families will require a competent law firm for this aspect of their wealth management. What is most important is that the family has a well-orchestrated team with all the appropriate disciplines represented.

- *Does the firm have the resources, expertise, and business model to support the family in strategic as well as tactical wealth management?* Will it assist in developing a family mission statement that reflects the family's values? If so, what process will it use? Will the firm or team of advisors help the family develop a family educational program that will identify future leaders and teach them to manage wealth? Do the people who will be involved have the expertise and experience to support the family in creating a decision-making process or framework for family governance? How will family communications be handled initially and on an ongoing basis?

  How will the advisors integrate the strategic and tactical issues for the benefit of the family? Can they share examples or references of how they have integrated these key elements for other clients?

- *How are team members compensated?* On product sales? Do they have goals for loans, deposits, or assets under management? Do they earn fees on basis points for asset management? Is the firm compensated hourly or by project? Does it work on retainer? Are the team members on commission, salary, or a combination of both? Does the firm offer a team-based compensation program, or is each team member paid on individual performance metrics? How is success defined for the team?

  These details are important. Families want to be certain that the advisors they select are aligned with the family goals for long-term wealth management and sustainability. They also want to ensure that their advisors are not at cross-purposes with one another. The family may have strong preferences about wealth management, and those preferences must be taken into account so that all the relationships—both inside and outside the family—work smoothly.

- *What is the total fee arrangement?* Does the firm have any hidden fees or other sources of revenue? Do the advisors accept any kind of compensation from any product providers? If yes, it's possible the family may be steered into products that provide revenue for the firm, but perhaps are not best for the client. Money talks. How does the firm handle potential conflicts of interest in fee structures and advisor compensation?
- *What is the standard client experience?* How often and under what circumstances can the family expect to hear from its advisors? Are there regular family meetings or retreats? If a family has current advisors they like, how will the firm communicate with those advisors, and who will take the leadership role? Will clients have immediate online access to their accounts, reports, and other information so they don't have to call the firm and wait for critical data? How is confidential information protected? Does the family have an opportunity to meet and network with other similar and like-minded families?
- *What role does the firm envision the family will play in coordinating the advisory team and the family?* It's important that the family divides roles and responsibilities among family members and family office employees, if any, to ensure accountability, coordination, and streamlined operation without duplicative efforts. Every member of the family also must feel that his or her interests are fairly represented.

When all these questions are answered, there's yet one more. How comfortable does the family feel with the people who will comprise their advisory team? As one family member put it, "I looked for assistance almost immediately after the merger of our company. I spoke with one highly regarded advisor who would be backed by a team of other experts. Technically, this man might have been superb, but he was condescending and treated me as if I couldn't possibly know anything about business. I didn't like that, and neither did my husband.

"Apparently, this potential advisor hadn't acquainted himself with the fact that my husband and I built the business together. My husband was the big-picture guy, and I handled the details. I must have done it well because the due diligence people from the company who bought us out said it was a very smooth process because of my painstaking recordkeeping over the past twenty years. But I was treated like an idiot with no understanding of anything this man might recommend.

"If he'd done *his* due diligence about his potential client, he would have known that I was an officer and key decision maker in the company. He didn't get the job, and my husband and I found a female advisor who was equally qualified. We're both very satisfied with her."

Whether it is an ultra-high-net-worth family who has inherited for generations or an entrepreneur who has created great wealth, it's essential to have a high-quality advisory team that can manage the family's integrated wealth management requirements. For some families the best choice may be to set up a family office, but such an arrangement comes with challenges and can be very expensive to structure and maintain. Chapter 5 will discuss the risks and opportunities of setting up a single or multifamily office.

Entrepreneurs who have given their lives to building a family business may be surprisingly unsophisticated about the best courses of action to take following a liquidity event. Although they might have been quite adept at running the business, they sometimes feel at sea after the business is gone and that they are drowning in a tidal wave of new responsibilities and reporting requirements.

Often they see wealth management simply as a set of tactics that must be implemented and maintained. Once their advisors have been chosen, documents drawn, and investments made, they may feel that their wealth-planning project has been completed. Although they understand that the program will need to be monitored and adjusted occasionally, for them the major part of the process is over. However, the fact is that their work is only partially finished. If the family has neglected the strategic dimensions of wealth management, it will likely not achieve long-term success.

For example, ten years ago, Dan Randal* sold his family farm in South Dakota for nearly $100 million to an energy syndicate. Dan's father had established the farm, and Dan had added to it meticulously over several decades.

At the time of the sale, Dan set up a family investment partnership for his wife and children, made investments including the purchase of a small jet that he piloted, and set off with his wife, Trish,* to see parts of the world they'd always wanted to visit. The farm had taken virtually all his time until it was sold, and Dan and his wife were having a wonderful adventure, enjoying what his constant efforts had made possible. "The kids were taken care of, I'd worked all my life, and this was our time. We loved every second of it."

Dan's son, Rick,* who was eighteen at the time of the sale, was now a twenty-eight-year-old pediatrician in a large group practice in another city. His daughter, Grace,* was a talented, though struggling, twenty-four-year-old jewelry designer, living across the country with a young man who was making

---

*The examples with an asterisk mentioned in this chapter are composites of cases the author has encountered in his wealth management career. Names and all identifying details have been changed to protect privacy.

a name as a portrait painter. Much of the children's money was managed in the family partnership. The children were happy in their lives, and Dan and Trish had more than enough money to continue their odyssey of discovery throughout the world.

Everything was going well for the family until Rick announced he wanted to marry Emily, an anesthesiologist he'd met in medical school. Neither family was surprised. Rick and Emily had been together for several years and had shared holidays and other special occasions with both his family and hers. Everyone was pleased and excited.

Dan's attorney, Harold Whitely,* a member of the law firm that had advised Dan on the sale of the farm, suggested to Dan that Rick and Emily should enter into a prenuptial agreement since Rick had substantial assets as a result of his interest in the family partnership. When Dan and Harold presented the idea to Rick, he was not in favor of it. In all the time he and Emily were together, he never discussed this idea with her. Now that they were engaged, Rick felt it was the wrong time to spring it on her.

However, at his father's urging, he agreed to mention the prenup to her. Emily was taken aback, then hurt, then furious. She felt that Rick's family, with whom she had been so close, now didn't trust her and considered her a golddigger, even though she had never known the extent of Rick's fortune.

Rick, too, was angry, feeling that he and Emily had been sandbagged. Nonetheless, he now realized just how wealthy he was, and he saw the wisdom of protecting his unexpectedly substantial fortune. He tried to convince Emily that the prenup also included safeguards for her, but she refused to sign. "I feel as if they're telling me that the only family that matters is the blood family. If I'm not blood, then I'm not really family. I might be an extension of the family, and my children would be members of the family, but I am and will always be an outlier. That's not acceptable to me at all. If I marry into a family, then I *am* a member of the family, not an interloper." Her relationship with the entire family, including Rick, soured, and she broke the engagement.

Although the pain was visited on Rick and Emily, the mistake was Dan's. He had not spent the time and resources necessary to prepare and educate his children about the risks, responsibilities, and challenges that come with wealth. He never communicated his values or preferences. He had not planned for the issues that wealth would create, nor had he given any attention to the prospect of in-law children or grandchildren and the potentially exponential growth of the family.

Had he done so, he and his advisors would have developed a plan to prepare Rick and Grace at the time the family sold the farm and created the family investment partnership. At sixteen and eighteen years of age, the children would have begun to learn not only how to manage wealth and the responsibilities and opportunities that come with it, but also would have heard the history of the farm and what it meant to Dan. They could have explored their parents' values and shared their own, thus beginning to form a cohesive sense of legacy. Dan, Trish, and their advisors would have involved both children in discussions about the family's future and educated them about how the money they would inherit could be managed and increased to support the family's hopes and dreams, not only in their own generation, but also for several to come.

Rick would have known the details of his assets, holdings, and investments. He would have heard about prenuptial agreements, and the benefits to both him and his fiancée would have been spelled out. He would have been taught how to raise and discuss the issue with a potential spouse.

This constant conversation and training should have been part of his growing up, not sprung on him suddenly, diluting and eventually destroying his relationship with a young woman he loved. His financial trust would not have become an occasion for personal mistrust.

In short, Dan had neglected the strategic dimensions of wealth planning, and the wounds were slow to heal. These kinds of misunderstandings and arguments are, unfortunately, typical when wealth planning includes only tactical issues.

The Elements of Business Planning versus Strategic Wealth Planning

A business generally comprises the management team, the employees, and the shareholders. For the business to run effectively, each constituent group has a specific role to play. Management leads the business, creates the business plan, and oversees execution. Employees are accountable to management and have responsibility for executing the operation of the business plan. Shareholders are the owners of the business, and management is accountable to them for effectively and efficiently running the business and reporting results.

The business of wealth for families who decide to manage their assets collectively has many similarities to a family or closely held operating business. There is generally a patriarch and/or matriarch who are equivalent to the management team. Family or nonfamily members who manage the wealth enterprise day by day are similar to employees while family members who do not work in the management of the wealth but have considerable interest in how it is handled can be roughly equated to shareholders. As in an operating business, these groups are bound by a common purpose and work together, sharing resources such as assets and revenue.

Successful entrepreneurs take part in strategic planning and execution as a necessary component of managing their business. As the following table indicates, the same planning and execution are essential for managing the business of family.

Strategic Plan/Tactics for an Operating Family Business	Strategic Plan/Tactics for a Family Wealth Enterprise
Developing a vision and mission for the business	Developing the vision and mission for use of the family wealth
Setting goals and objectives that support the vision and mission	Setting goals and objectives that advance the vision and mission
Defining roles and responsibilities for employees	Defining family members' roles and responsibilities for managing the wealth of the family enterprise
Identifying and educating leaders	Identifying current and future family leaders
Planning for succession	Creating a succession plan to manage changes in leadership
Training employees	Providing wealth management information and education for the family
Initiating comprehensive communication planning	Initiating a plan for regular, clear, and useful communication between and among the family members
Setting up the tactical plans that support the business strategy	Setting up annual tactical plans and reviews that support the overall strategic plan for the family's wealth

The needs of each constituent group must be attended to and balanced for the family enterprise to run smoothly and with a minimum level of conflict. In his book, James Hughes states that the assets of a family are its individual members.[4] If he is right, those assets must be safeguarded, cared for, and kept in good repair if the family enterprise is to grow and thrive beyond the current generation. A strategic scaffold is a must.

If members of a family decide to manage their wealth as a group, they must learn to trust one another, and nothing builds trust like honest, frank, and frequent communication among nuclear family members and the wider family enterprise. No matter how much DNA they share, each family member is different from every other member. A sister may be a risk taker; her brother may be more cautious. One cousin may be a natural networker while another is a lone wolf. Some members of the family are glass-half-full thinkers; others are deeply pessimistic. Some are spenders, and some are stewards. The same family may encompass pillars of the church and atheists, introverts and extroverts, and arts lovers and sports fanatics.

Each family may have different ideas about how the wealth should be used. A son may want to invest in new business opportunities that bring jobs and strengthen the economy of a city. His brother would rather support the city through direct philanthropy. Throw in the in-law children and their children, who can be close friends or unknown to one another, and it becomes evident that family communication webs are complex and rife with opportunities for disagreements.

Nevertheless, it is clearly beneficial for families to incorporate a well-defined method of communication to sustain wealth and maintain positive and effective family relationships based on trust, clarity, and understanding.

Notes

1. Gregory T. Rogers, D. Scott Budge, and Lauris S. Lambergs, "Managing Issues of Ultra High Net Worth Clients: Conference Offers Some Suggestions," Wealth Management.com (December 1, 2014), wealthmanagement.com/high-net-worth/managing-issues-ultra-high-net-worth-clients. Retrieved February 19, 2016.
2. Ibid.
3. www.investopedia.com.
4. James E. Hughes Jr., *Family Wealth: Keeping It in the Family* (New York: Bloomberg Press, 2004), pp. 16–17.

CHAPTER 5

Should We Manage Wealth as a Family?

Whether to manage wealth as a family collective is an important and complex decision. Careful consideration has to be given to the nature of the wealth, the legal structure of ownership, the roles and responsibilities of the family members, the relationships among the key constituents, and their shared and independent values, goals, and objectives, among other factors.

From reading Chapter 4, you may have come to the conclusion that managing wealth as an all-family consortium is the only road to take. That's not necessarily the case. For some families, the best decision is for each member to manage his or her own wealth based on independent goals and preferences.

Among the myriad reasons a family might choose to go it alone are:

- Individual families within the group have differing ideas about the use of wealth, and after considerable discussion, the rest of the family doesn't appear to be flexible enough to accommodate these divergent ideas.
- Individual family members have very distinct investment objectives, time horizons, risk tolerances, and preferences and cannot find a consistent approach that meets everyone's requirements.
- Family members have local investment opportunities through their own networks that they cannot or do not want to share with everyone in the family.
- Family members have engaged trusted advisors they wish to keep and have no desire to involve another group.
- An individual family prefers privacy rather than sharing personal information with other family members who may be no closer than cousins and with whom they are only slightly acquainted.

51

- The family has agreed that "family" encompasses only lineal descendants of the wealth creator. In-laws are not included, and their family-member spouses may not appreciate the second-class status accorded their husbands or wives.
- The family is widely dispersed across the country or the world.

However, many families with very significant resources can realize substantial benefits from managing the wealth in a centralized manner. These benefits include cost savings, relationship pricing, and access to distinctive investment offerings. In addition, they can realize economies of scale in working with outside advisors, hiring employees, and leveraging technology. The benefits families can achieve through managing wealth as an enterprise parallels the significant growth of single and multifamily offices over the last two decades. Today there are approximately 3,000 single-family offices in the United States and about 150 multifamily offices.[1]

For example, many compelling investments, particularly in the alternative investment arena such as private placement, absolute return funds, and private equity funds, require a minimum investment of $1 million to $5 million or more. Often individual family members either cannot or do not wish to invest that much in one fund or investment opportunity. However, if they spread the investment among the family—along with many types of other investments—they can enjoy the positive benefits while still managing risk through diversification.

In addition, most investment funds and managers offer a graduated fee schedule that reduces the basis points they charge on higher asset levels. Since fees can be a significant drag on investment returns, lowering them can help improve results.

Along with increasing the efficiency and effectiveness of a family's investment portfolio, sharing resources can decrease individual expenses and provide more consistency and efficiency. All family members of an ultra-high-net-worth family need information management, tax planning and compliance, payment of expenses and distributions of income, financial planning, risk management, insurance protection, and property management. Each of these activities requires professional support, technology, and other resources that can be shared across the family to improve effectiveness through a centralized approach.

However, to be successful in the collective approach to managing wealth, families must work together to define the roles and responsibilities of each family member, along with any potential family employees or professional advisors. The family also must determine an effective and efficient communication plan that supports the needs of each family member. Sharing ownership of family assets can make financial sense, but sometimes can be tricky to navigate.

For example, Ken Wilson's* grandfather passed away two years ago, and in accordance with the terms of the grandfather's trust, Ken's share of his grandfather's estate was $32 million. Ken lives in Hawaii with his wife and six children, who are seventeen, sixteen, fifteen, thirteen, eleven, and eight years of age. The rest of the extended family resides in Portland, Maine. The family has chosen to manage the grandfather's wealth as a collective. Ken has opted not to.

"It just doesn't work for me," Ken says. "I love my family. Everyone is on very good terms, but they want to have quarterly meetings in Boston and family retreats every other year, too. I have my own business to run, which involves lots of late hours and weekends, and the kids are very active in sports, music, theater, and school clubs. I can't see taking the entire family of eight back to the mainland several times a year, and if I go myself, I'll probably end up missing the kids' games and other activities. I've been so busy over the years my family has sometimes felt as if they were taking a back seat, and I'm going to make sure that doesn't continue.

"With the distribution from my grandfather's estate, I can widen the scope of my business and hand over some of my duties to new officers. I can build the business while increasing my time with the family. Two of the kids will be going off to college soon, and I want to have some adventures with them before that happens.

"I've elected to take my share of the estate and manage it from here. I'll use the money to advance my objectives as I see fit. Some of the things my family wants to invest in, I don't. Living where I do, I have a pretty keen interest in environmental issues and like to invest in that sector. Some of the family, while socially responsible, doesn't want to put much of the family money into things I value. They offered to break out a portion of the family wealth for me and let me invest that myself, but that solution somehow felt like they were just placating me.

"I know I may miss out on some benefits of the wealth being concentrated and coordinated, but geographically, all these family meetings and get-togethers don't make sense for me at this time of my life. I'm sure I can find the right advisors here in Hawaii. I'm very grateful for my grandfather's planning, but I'll take it from here."

---

*The examples with an asterisk mentioned in this chapter are composites of cases the author has encountered in his wealth management career. Names and all identifying details have been changed to protect privacy.

Family Offices: Will You Need One?

The Family Office Exchange notes that "the family office is a unique family business that is created to provide tailored wealth management solutions (from investments to philanthropy) in an integrated fashion while promoting and preserving the identity and values of the family."[2]

A single-family office (SFO) is an organization designed and managed to administer and oversee the family wealth management issues for one family. In an article for *Forbes*, Todd Ganos describes the SFO as "an organization that assumes the day-to-day administration and management of a family's affairs. To that end, to honestly call itself a family office, an organization needs to provide more than just the standard wealth management functions."[3]

Beyond the typical wealth management activities—taxes, private banking, recordkeeping, and other day-to-day assistance—many single-family offices increasingly offer what are called concierge services for families whose lives are particularly complex. In those cases, the office may handle the family's travel arrangements and sometimes even hires, or at least screens, applicants for domestic staff positions. They might manage an extensive art collection, keeping the family informed of changes in value or an opportunity to purchase a particular piece that will fill an important niche. In short, the family office handles the finances and anything else necessary to simplify or enrich life for its clients.

As a family ages, the family office involvement may go even further as members of the office are called upon to assist with delicate situations such as a family member's developing dementia or coping with other vicissitudes of growing older. The office may be involved in finding a contractor or builder to retrofit the family home with an elevator, a first-floor master suite, walk-in bathing facilities, or other amenities that allow family members to age in place. If this is not possible, they may join forces with the family to research appropriate alternative living arrangements. Obviously, these situations encompass both financial and social dimensions that may necessitate adjustments in planning. They also require tact, good judgment, and absolute confidentiality.

In short, SFOs can be useful centralized organizational structures for managing and transferring wealth from generation to generation and for increasing efficiency in comparison to each family member's handling these requirements on its own. As a family grows and its needs change, so do the services it requires, and an SFO may be well-suited to help guide the entire family through the evolutions that sometimes accompany great wealth. They also offer the family the greatest control over its assets, resources, and destiny.

However, single-family offices are not inexpensive propositions. Experts recommend that families have at least $250 million—and in some cases up to

$1 billion—to make a full-featured family office a viable option. The expenses of running the office typically cost as much as $1 million per year or more, which limits their effectiveness to most of those who are not among the world's top-tier wealthy.

The major expenses include hiring a staff of professionals; buying, maintaining, and continually upgrading the technology necessary to support the services the family requires; providing the research tools that inform the family office team about changes to the complex issues they will oversee; gathering the resources necessary to maintain compliance and regulatory standards; and providing and maintaining office space for family office team members.

Multifamily offices (MFOs) may make more sense for those clients who wish to reduce costs and do not want the administrative responsibilities of an SFO. Multifamily offices provide financial, tax, legal, and the other family office services to a group of ultra-high-net-worth families who decide not to establish a single-family office, but still want access to specialized services. They also provide introductions to similar families for networking, sharing experiences, and co-investing. Additionally, MFOs, because of their scale and the number of families they represent, often offer entrée to products and services that are beyond the scope of most SFOs.

In the past, MFOs grew from SFOs, as the members of the single-family office discovered the economies of scale that could be realized by allowing others into the group. Today, however, multifamily offices also have been established by banks, brokerages, and professional groups. MFOs offer a good alternative to SFOs, and many quality firms offer this service.

The First Family Office — and a Mistake

An embedded family office is sometimes the first step a family takes toward managing its wealth. The office, embedded in the family business, calls upon the talents of employees who work in the business to take over the management of financial activities that typically would be handled by an independent family office on behalf of the wealth owners.

When a business grows, thrives, and creates wealth for the founders, the owners often have both corporate management responsibilities and increasing personal wealth management requirements. It seems to make sense for them to turn over some of the duties of administering their personal finances to trusted employees who support their business, which is generally their largest asset. After all, the employees are skilled at their work and have proven their loyalty to the family. The size of the embedded office may range from one person handling financial and legal matters to several employees working on

THE EMBEDDED FAMILY OFFICE: CAUTIONS

The Family Office Exchange lists the following features that are typical of an embedded family office:

- There is a department within the company referred to as "shareholder relations."
- Certain employees are dedicated solely to working with the family without other business-related responsibilities.
- There is a separate physical space, often at the company's headquarters, that houses employees working on family matters.
- Employees interact directly with the family's outside financial advisors on personal financial matters.
- Family members are billed directly for time spent by the business employees on personal financial matters.
- The company's IT department is used to set up personal devices and serve as a "help desk" for family members.
- Family member tax returns are coordinated by the company's Tax or Accounting Departments.

Source: The Family Office Exchange, "Do You Have an Embedded Family Office?"[4]

various aspects of the family's financial planning, investments, accounting, and tax issues.

Even if the family office employees are segregated from others in the company, they are still employees, and commingling family and business matters can create problems and increase risk for the family.

Jealousy can infect both employees and family. Other company employees may feel that these "family" employees have preferred status. Their reactions can range from vague feelings of annoyance all the way to passive-aggressive sabotage. In addition, family members who don't work in the business may feel that the relatives who are part of the business have a leg up by having daily contact with these advisors.

Confidentiality is a big concern. The employees tasked with family responsibilities are privy to both business and personal information about members of the family—and people talk. Where they talk and what they disclose, even carelessly and without malice, can spread throughout the company like wildfire. Everything from a stock pick to an impending divorce can find its way onto the grapevine—and from there to other grapevines outside the company. In the world of social media, the grapevine is worldwide, and rumors that end up on the web can be harder to refute than ever before. Even if the revelation of family information doesn't prove to be devastating, private matters should remain private, and this way of managing wealth increases chances for a public airing of sensitive family intelligence.

Also, if the business is the victim of a cybersecurity breach or other fraudulent activity, both the operations and the family are affected, and untangling the interwoven financial ramifications may take a very long time.

Having a great deal of company and family information in the hands of a few people can be a knotty issue. Suppose the executive handling both corporate and family finances is lured away by another company, or worse, becomes incapacitated or dies. Who else in the company has the knowledge of both financial spheres? As the search for records and reports goes on, the result is confusion both in the company and the family—and it may take months for both to recover.

A stickier problem is whether the employees tapped for the family office are the right ones. Just because an employee is skilled in one area, he or she may not be equally conversant with another. For example, even a company CFO with major responsibilities for planning, operations, and risk management may not be the person to handle the family's portfolio of investments or even to make other wealth management recommendations and decisions. He or she may not have enough expertise in such areas as setting objectives for investments or laying out the strategy for creating, analyzing, or diversifying the family's assets. Yet, the CFO is often the person asked to carry out these duties, possibly with varying degrees of success. It takes only one major mistake to have an equally major impact on the business and the family's wealth.

It's possible that if the CFO is providing investment advice, he or she might be operating as a registered investment advisor without, in fact, being registered with the SEC or state securities authorities—and that ambiguity can cause problems if the investment activities are scrutinized.

Problems with taxes can bring business to a standstill and seriously damage or destroy a company's reputation and valuation. If one person is doing two jobs—one for the company and one for the family—the tax ramifications can be enormous. In an article for *Family Office Review*, Shanaz Mahmoud points out, "If you are a sole owner of a company and none of the employees have a bonus or qualified plan ... all of this is fine—except you can't deduct those expenses because they are personal expenses. If you do, you are violating tax law and filing fraudulently."[5]

In addition, if an employee is spending a certain percentage of his time working for the family and the rest for the business, the business owner must separate the two functions for tax purposes—and time lost to this additional tax compliance is wasted time that could be spent on revenue generation or other more important tasks. The greater the number of employees who split their time, the more complex the accounting becomes, the more time is required, and the greater the chance of running afoul of a state tax regulation.

In addition, various state or federal workplace regulations are affected by how the employee's time is divided. If an accounting error is made, even innocently, the penalties could be significant. Regulatory problems also can open up the company to further audit and scrutiny to determine how the business is being run. Some of those with a vested interest in the results of the investigation may be the family members who are outside the business but believe they are being damaged by the decisions of the family members inside the business. Unfortunately, sloppy governance of the operating business can be the opening salvo in a bloody, years-long internecine war.

Another reason embedded offices are not the most effective approach is that the employees chosen to work for the family are concentrating almost exclusively on money; that is, they are performing the tasks of tactical wealth management. They may be aware of problems with family and business dynamics, but in all probability, they have neither the training nor the power to address let alone solve them.

The ultimate solution is to separate family wealth management from the management of the business that generated the wealth in the first place—and to integrate strategic and tactical wealth management into a holistic program that addresses not only the assets but also the family who holds them. This separation keeps things cleaner, and the family is free to choose not only advisors with expertise in the tactical areas but also those with vast knowledge of the strategic dimensions. They may choose to set up a family office of some type or select a group of wealth management advisors who work together as a cohesive team to seek the best solutions for all the conundrums that attend extensive holdings and great wealth.

Even if the family has chosen advisors wisely, the duties of strategic wealth management must be split between the professionals and the family. It is the family, not an outside consultant, who must decide on the model it wants to foster today and in the future. Family members also are ultimately responsible for making critical decisions about stewardship and how the next—and succeeding—generations will be prepared for family leadership. The advisors have the resources at hand to help the family accomplish what it's set out to do, but the family must chart the course.

The family knows the strengths and weaknesses of each member better than anyone else. For example, Todd Mitchell* and his brother Christopher* built a very successful regional shopping mall that was bought out several years ago by a large real estate developer for more than $500 million. The second generation includes Todd's children, Edward* and Lauren,* and Christopher's son and daughter, Jerry* and Alix.* The brothers live in the same town and remain very close. Their children grew up more like siblings than cousins; they are still friends today, and the entire family is remarkably free of discord.

Todd and Christopher invested wisely, but are now thinking beyond immediate needs. Although they gave their children large cash gifts when the buyout was concluded, they now wish to be more intentional about the future. They have hired an advisory firm to help them plan for successful wealth management and transfer in an effort to create a sustainable family legacy.

To the outside advisor, Jerry seems to be the most financially savvy member of the second generation. Charismatic and charming, he talks a good game, but the first generation of wealth builders knows he's only been following the advice of his cousin Lauren, who's a thoughtful, successful investor. She has built an enviable portfolio that allowed her to weather the Great Recession of 2008 with little damage to her personal fortune.

Although his investment success and gift of gab might make it appear that Jerry is the logical choice to convey information to and from the investment advisor, the family prefers Lauren because they know the backstory. Although she may be less verbally adroit than her cousin, the family selects her for this important role.

In the course of discussion with the advisors, other roles are sorted out. Alix, for example, is a domestic relations attorney and brings negotiating skills to the table. Jerry, it turns out, loves research, and would be happy to search the family history back beyond his father and uncle, while Edward is a teacher who can assist in bringing the eleven members of the third generation into the process as they become old enough.

Obviously, the Mitchell family is lucky. The wealth creators are close, the cousins love and respect one another, and the family members all still live within an hour's drive of each other. It's a tight-knit unit, eager to work together. They have similar goals and little conflict.

It's not always that way. Sibling rivalries and grievances can be intense, making the second generation prone to distrust. Even if they agree on wealth management concepts, day-to-day cooperation can be hard to achieve. If these conflicts are carried over into the third generation, things can fall apart rapidly—shirtsleeves to shirtsleeves. The tendency can be exacerbated by the fact that families, who in the past often lived in the same town, now live in different states or even different countries. The distance between them can loosen the family bonds considerably.

Each generation models behavior for the next. If previous generations have kept the family story alive, engaged in civil discussion of critical and sometimes difficult issues, encouraged consensus building, and identified the factors that all—or at least most—family members hold in common, then the chances for success are improved.

Notes

1. Capgemini, "The Global State of Family Offices: What Family Offices Need to Do to Successfully Compete with Wealth Traditional Management Firms," www.cn.capgemini.com/resource-file-access/resource/pdf/The_Global_State_of _Family_Offices.pdf. Retrieved March 17, 2016.
2. Family Office Exchange website, "Starting a Family Office," https://www.family office.com/knowledge-center/starting-family-office.Retrieved March 4, 2016.
3. Todd Ganos, "What Is a Family Office?" *Forbes* (August 13, 2013). Retrieved March 4, 2016.
4. Do you have an embedded family office? https://www.familyoffice.com/insights/ do-you-have-embedded-family-of%EF%AC%81ce. Retrieved March 7, 2016.
5. Shanaz Mahmoud, "To Embed or Go Virtual with Your Family Office: That Is the Question," http://www.astonpearl.com/press/2013/Family-office-8-6-13.pdf, August 6, 2013. Retrieved March 7, 2016.

CHAPTER 6

The Story of Wealth Creation: Why It Matters

Every wealth creation event has a story behind it, and it is in those stories we find the seeds that have germinated and blossomed into a family history and culture. The stories mean nothing, however, if they are lost in the mists of time. They must be preserved, revisited, and kept alive through family sharing if they are to inform successive generations.

Storytelling itself is as old as human language. Even today, both ancient and modern cultures pass on knowledge through oral traditions. In the stories told from generation to generation, listeners learn and absorb the history, values, customs, and rituals revered by a society, clan, or family. These factors shape the way in which the group makes decisions, defines the world around them, and develops a vision for the future. The individual and collective events and influences of the family create the values of the current generation. Those values provide the seeds for the family's vision of the future. For families with significant resources that have the possibility of lasting through generations, the wealth or the stories behind it bind the family together. Without the context of the wealth history, the family story is about nothing but money. The truth is, however, that wealth is more than money, and history is more than wealth.

The Family Narrative

Perhaps the strongest tie holding a family together is its shared story—and yet many family members know nothing about their pasts beyond their grandparents. In fact, if you ask the majority of Americans about their great-grandparents, they generally know very little, if anything, about them. They usually are removed from current family members by only two to three generations, but in most cases the great-grandparents' stories are unknown or forgotten by the current generations.

Society itself can create barriers to sustaining a family's shared sense of history and identity. Branches of the family may live in different states, regions, and even countries. They may have been widely separated for so long they wouldn't know each other if they passed on the street. In addition, with the proliferation of social media, on-demand entertainment, and the communication of news and information through personal devices, contemporary culture has become an increasingly individualized rather than a collective experience.

Technologies such as Skype, FaceTime, and others have made it easier for family members to keep in touch, but these advancements are not always conducive to meaningful dialogue about matters of substance. While it may be true that as a society we have never been more connected, it's also true that in some ways we have never been less in touch. Although we would not wish to romanticize the past, in earlier times, families often lived in the same cities for generations and their stories and values were well-known to the entire clan.

In spite of these impediments to unity, successful multigenerational families of wealth usually have developed and preserved an ethos based on a strong and well-understood history of the family and a knowledge of the wealth creation story. They understand that their wealth is not only the assets they possess.

As Daniell and Hamilton say, "Family ... is far more than a static family tree of past births, deaths, and marriages. [It] is, in essence, the sum of valued accomplishments, traditions, assets, histories, experiences, lives, places, and memories that flow from the past through the present and into the future."[1]

It's clear, then, that history matters. It is a tragedy that so much of it is lost. When working with clients, I sometimes ask them if they are aware of their great-grandparents' stories—the struggles they had and whether or not they had been able to overcome them. Were there outstanding successes about which they had heard? Do they know the names of all their great-grandparents' children beyond their own grandparents? The result is too often silence. I then ask, "What do you want your great-grandchildren to know about you?"

The response to this question is always much more voluble. They want their descendants to understand the toil, the setbacks, the successes, and the joys the wealth creator experienced in providing assets not only for himself and his nuclear family, but also for the family as a whole. They don't want their story to be lost as their great-grandparents' has been. They hope the values they espouse are embedded in the family now and in the future. They want to leave a legacy that lasts for generations. They want to make a difference. They want to matter.

Why the Family History Should Be Told to Children, Too

In his article, "The Family Stories That Bind Us," Bruce Feiler cites the work of psychologist Marshall Duke, who discovered that "the more children knew about their family's history, the stronger their sense of control over their lives, the higher their self-esteem and the more successfully they believed their families functioned. . . . The children with the most self-confidence have what Duke calls a 'strong intergenerational self.'"[2]

When Feiler's article was published, Duke himself took to print to clarify some aspects of his research. In an article for *The Huffington Post*, he indicated that simply teaching children facts about their families was not enough to make them stronger. "Rather," he said, "it is our belief that knowledge of family history reflects certain processes that exist in families whose members know their histories. One such process is *the communication of family information across generations*"[3] (Italics mine). In short, storytelling, which can be enhanced by other aspects of family life: traditions, symbols and rituals, experiences, iconography and mottos, and even heirlooms, to name a few.

It stands to reason that families in which the majority of children come up possessing a powerful intergenerational self will maintain considerable cohesion even as older members of the family die and new ones are born. Stories have power, and as they are retold intergenerationally, the power of the stories grows with the telling.

Beyond feeling a strong internal locus of control and sense of connectedness, children who know their family histories also are more resilient than those who don't. This resilience, if shared by the majority of members, stands a family in good stead when hardships arise—which occurs in all families because wealth does not inoculate against sorrow, loss, pain, illness, aging, injury, or just plain bad luck. If all generations have come to learn their family history, they can set those untoward events into a broader landscape and move forward with greater confidence than those who have little sense of who they are and what they stand for.

For example, in an article for the *Wall Street Journal*, Peter Jaskiewicz and James G. Combs reported on research they conducted on entrepreneurial German winemaking families who had been in business for generations. Among the group they studied, the average winery had been in the same family since the 1700s and the longest winery-owning family encompassed thirty-three generations, beginning in the tenth century. The authors identified five traits they felt were essential for entrepreneurial as opposed to traditional families. Of those traits, the first is the transmission of the family history.

"[These families]," the authors said, "have what we call an 'Entrepreneurial Legacy' that is passed from each generation to the next. . . . Stories . . . put current risks and problems in a broader context. It is hard to complain about losing a customer knowing your great-grandparents overcame war and starvation to build the business."[4]

Telling It All

Uncovering family history and placing today's family within it is a good thing. The wealth creator's values and lessons are important in shaping the family's future goals and mission. Yet most wealth creators admit they couldn't have done it without the help and support of a spouse, partner, or even another member of the family. Wealth creation often requires a considerable amount of time away from the family, leaving to others the responsibilities for child rearing, establishing values and rituals, or participating in the community to build the public reputation and legacy of a family. Those stories are worth telling, too.

As the generations rise and fall, they must not be hemmed in by what James Hughes calls the gravitational pull of "the founding dream."[5] While the *values* of the family may endure, the *wealth* must serve the purposes of the members who are here today and those who will follow. As Hughes says, "A founder's dream is an extraordinary and impressive expression of human capital. . . . But [these dreams] by their power may prevent future dreams from being born. In such cases, human capital destroys itself."[6]

In other words, the founder's dream may inform the succeeding generations, but it must not dictate their lives. By placing the wealth creator's story in the context of a longer narrative, and by including the stories of those from other branches of the tree, generations of heirs can identify with the panoply of personalities who ultimately produced the wealth creator and come to value each person's contribution to the greater family legacy.

Very few families' histories feature an unbroken upward trajectory. People are human. They stumble. They make bad decisions. They fall prey to any number of failings, such as multiple marriages and divorces, substance abuse, and even criminal behavior. The family business might have been built on a combination of laudable ethical choices and sharp dealings at the edge of legality.

The less-than-honorable parts of the story may make the family squirm, but resilient families soldier on, incorporating the lessons learned from adversity and transforming the corrections into points of pride. Success simply teaches us what we already know, offering little opportunity for learning. Failure, on the other hand, is the point at which human beings begin to acquire new knowledge. Working through mishaps and reversals is the catalyst for growth. A terrible mistake may, in fact, be the cornerstone of a whole new family structure. As Dr. Henry Louis Gates Jr. noted on his PBS series *Finding Your Roots*, "Untold stories [are] buried in the past . . . overlooked. These recovered stories can, for a new generation, become a source of inspiration and pride."

Omitting the traumas and tragedies of the family history does damage to the truth and robs successive generations of the lessons of triumph and overcoming—and when challenging events threaten to destabilize a family, those lessons are the most valuable of all.

Recovering the Legacy

Today, the proliferation of genealogy websites and the growing number of users attest to the fact that people are hungry to know who they are and where they came from. The best *place* to learn is through the extended family, and the best *way* to learn is by sharing the stories passed down from generation to generation. Although creating the family tree from a genealogical site is a fascinating exercise in itself, uncovering the stories of the people who came before strengthens the roots, and listening to stories told directly by those who lived them puts the leaves on the tree. Whether the stories are told informally around the dinner table or are part of a structured family meeting, real history told by real people brings immediacy to what otherwise might be a dry recitation of facts.

Involving multiple generations in capturing and sharing the family history contributes to long-term cohesion over a shared past. Some families begin this search for stories by asking the third generation—the ones who may be at risk of being the "shirtsleeve" generation because they are more removed from the efforts it took to build the wealth—to be responsible for interviewing the previous two generations and compiling the stories, which may go back several generations before the wealth creator's personal history.[7] Connecting these authentic tales from the elders may transform a lackadaisical third-generation member into a strong, proud family champion.

Even if the entire family is geographically dispersed, there's no reason family units cannot conduct such historical research and combine their results when they come together to work out the issues of wealth management.

Using these histories, families can begin to discern the attitudes and values that have been transmitted. Does the family cherish safety, entrepreneurship, public service, adventure, philanthropy, education, religion, a combination, or other characteristics? How have these tendencies been manifested throughout the generations? Which values and traits does the family wish to honor and nurture? Which ones need to be overcome for the long-term health of the family?

Some wealth creators, mindful of the legacy they initiated and wish to see carried on, may decide to make an ethical will. Oftentimes, these documents are videotaped and uploaded so the family has the experience of both seeing and hearing the wealth creator's story and vision for the future.

Different from a will that distributes assets, an ethical will has no force of law. It is instead a simple and direct way for the family patriarch or matriarch to share thoughts, hopes, and dreams with the family. Some choose to write such documents late in life, but they also may be communicated at other times in the heirs' experience. Ethical wills allow the writer to do the following:

- Articulate values and make plans to ensure they continue.
- Ensure that important stories are not forgotten as each branch of the family grows.
- Share important personal and/or spiritual beliefs as well as their love and affection with family members.
- Impart the lessons life has taught them and to offer helpful advice to the family as a whole or to a specific generation or person.

Author Pat McNees feels that the term *ethical* sounds "preachy and legalistic" and prefers alternatives such as "ending note," or "legacy letter."[8] These descriptions may more fully capture the intent of the document, which is to share stories and values with those who remain.

Once family stories are recovered, mechanisms must be in place to memorialize them. While many families choose to put the information in writing for easy retrieval, some families place these documents on a USB drive or store them in the cloud. How the information is kept is left to the family. What is most important is that the method selected be secure and easy to use. In many families, one or more family members have an interest in pursuing the family history and not only understand the value of this endeavor but also enjoy doing the work. It's an important role, and those who step forward to manage it should be applauded.

The family history need not be a novel. Focusing on an archival history that includes significant events, influences, and family or business milestones will be very valuable and digestible by current and future family members.

THE INITIAL QUESTIONS

Learning about their history prepares a family to plan its vision and mission statements. The following questions provide the framework for that discussion:

- What lessons, values, attributes, or opportunities helped the founder to create wealth?
- How closely do our family values correlate with those of the wealth creator? If we have veered away from those values, has that distance benefited the family, or should we reexamine the original values?
- What did, or does, money mean to the wealth creator? What does it mean to the rest of the family?
- What sacrifices did the founder and succeeding generations make to create the family fortune?
- Are there particular ideals, values, or purposes that are extremely important to the wealth creator or the current generation of wealth owners? What are they?
- What actions did the founder take to amass the wealth? Would the family want to emulate those actions today? If yes, how do we carry those actions forward in a new environment?
- Do all the family members subscribe to the same understanding of our legacy?

A Family Legacy

If ever there was a family whose legacy runs deep, it's the family of Rose Fitzgerald and Joseph P. Kennedy. The dark filaments of triumph, tragedy, infidelity, and scandal from generation to generation are tightly interwoven with the bright thread of exceptional public service. Although the Kennedys today are no longer one of America's richest families, their legacy of service continues unabated.

The Kennedy dining table, where the day's national and international events were discussed and dissected by adults and children alike, set the stage for both staggering hubris and exceptional accomplishments.

No matter what catastrophes depleted the family—assassinations and plane crashes taking the lives of four of the nine children—the Kennedys reached back into their history to find a way to transcend them. Although they were rich beyond the imagining of many, money was not the reason they survived. What saved the family again and again was a sense of legacy and a feeling of destiny. In the midst of pain, their public life continued—in the House of Representatives, the Senate, and the presidency—and though the current generation is not as active in national politics as those that went before, their influence in public service remains intact. Members of the fourth generation of American Kennedys include Ambassador to Japan Caroline Kennedy Schlossberg, documentarian Rory Kennedy, environmental activist Robert Kennedy Jr., and lawyer Kathleen Kennedy Townsend, the former lieutenant governor of Maryland. Joseph Patrick Kennedy III followed his father into the House of Representatives from Massachusetts, while Patrick J. Kennedy represented Rhode Island. Edward Kennedy Jr. serves in the state senate in Connecticut. The family is a testament to the power of history and remembrance.

A Legacy Lost — and Recaptured

Dominic Gardenia* faced a tough decision in selling three car dealerships that his grandfather Louis had founded almost fifty years ago in Springfield, Missouri. He never expected the offer from Autonation*, and when it came through, it was a significantly more than he anticipated. When the transaction closed, the family would receive almost $140 million after taxes. Dominic also believed in his heart that the auto industry was experiencing dramatic changes and it was the right time to sell. Furthermore, none of his children or his brother Rick's* or sister Kristine's* children showed any real interest in being involved in the dealerships.

Nevertheless, he felt the bigger-than-life shadow of his late grandfather standing behind him. Louis Gardenia's* life's work seemed to seep out of the walls of each dealership. In 1965, Louis had purchased the first one after working for the previous owner, Tom Fiore,* for almost twenty years. He had started his career sweeping floors and cleaning cars in 1947 after coming to the United States from Sicily shortly after the end of World War II. He barely spoke English, but he was handsome, charming, and persistent—and he talked Tom into giving him a job. During his tenure at Fiore Ford, he did every job in the dealership, finally working his way up to sales manager. Tom treated Lou like the son he never had, and when he was ready to retire, he offered Lou the chance to purchase the dealership. Lou did not have the money, but Tom believed in the man he had mentored and agreed to finance the sale to Lou.

Over the next twenty-two years, Lou successfully managed and developed his dealership. After it had grown much larger, he bought two more. By

---

*The examples with an asterisk mentioned in this chapter are composites of cases the author has encountered in his wealth management career. Names and all identifying details have been changed to protect privacy.

1985, he employed more than one hundred people and had become an icon in Springfield. Everyone knew his television commercials, which were notable for their humor and straight talk. Lou also was deeply involved in his community. He was a deacon at his church, the head of the Rotary Club, and a local leader of the Chamber of Commerce. He loved life and loved his community, and they loved him. When he retired in 1990, his son Vincent* took over as president, remaining until his retirement in 2004. He then passed the dealerships on to Dominic.

To Dom, his oldest grandchild, Lou was bigger than life. Lou was his role model and his mentor. As Dom sat in his office in January 2015, he felt conflicted. How could he sell the business that had meant so much and done so much for his grandfather and his family? It was Lou's legacy, and it was going to evaporate as the core holding and identity of the family. Because Lou had passed away before his great-grandchildren were born, they knew him only through the occasional stories they heard from Vincent, Dom, and other members of the family. Dom wondered how his children, his eventual grandchildren, and the generations that followed would ever understand the challenges, ingenuity, perseverance, and compassion that had been the catalyst for successful wealth creation.

As Dom was considering this transaction, he sought the counsel of his longstanding attorney, James Forester.* During their discussions of the sale, Dom confided in James his concerns about losing the legacy his grandfather had created and his fear that the current and future generations would never understand or appreciate everything that the family endured in creating this wealth. James suggested to Dom that he consider hiring a firm that specializes in documenting family histories. James had previously referred a couple of other clients to Dr. Susan Radcliff, PhD.* Susan was a historian who started a firm that helped families build archival histories in an effort to help them understand and preserve their family history while also building a legacy for generations to come.

Dom met with Susan and retained her to catalog and document the history of Gardenia Motors. Susan interviewed all the family members and many current and former employees of the company. She also researched all the photographs, articles, newspaper ads, and television commercials. With this great trove of information, she created a comprehensive family history. The process took about three months. Dom was very pleased with her work and finally felt comfortable about moving forward with the sale of the family business.

A couple of weeks after completing the family history, Dom and his siblings called a family meeting to share the details of the pending sale of the business with all their family members. During the meeting, Dom gave each of them a beautifully bound book about the business and the founder. He asked Susan to offer a brief presentation for the family, sharing some of the special stories and significant moments in the history of the business that illustrated the challenges, opportunities, and values it took to maintain and grow the business over fifty years. It was a very emotional moment for Dom and the rest of the family. There were few dry eyes in the room.

This process helped the family appreciate what Louis and the other families had done in building the business that created financial security and opportunity for current and future generations. This understanding helped members of the family bond over the heritage and feel a sense of ownership and responsibility in building the legacy for the future.

If the family history largely has been lost, a similar process can be useful in recapturing it. This history is valuable in forming the undergirding of the family mission statement and in answering the essential question about family wealth management, which will be discussed in Chapter 7.

Notes

1. Mark Haynes Daniell and Sarah S. Hamilton, *Family Legacy and Leadership: Preserving True Family Wealth in Challenging Times* (Asia: John Wiley & Sons, 2010), p. 10.
2. Bruce Feiler, "This Life, The Family Stories That Bind Us," *New York Times* (March 15, 2013), www.nytimes.com/2013/03/17/fashion/the-family-stories-that-bind-us-this-life.html?_r=0m. Retrieved March 23, 2016.
3. Marshall P. Duke, "The Stories That Bind Us: What Are the 20 Questions?" *Huffington Post* (March 23, 2013), www.huffingtonpost.com/marshall-p-duke/the-stories-that-bind-us-_b_2918975.html. Retrieved March 28, 2016.
4. Peter Jaskiewicz and James G. Combs, "How to Keep a Family Business Alive for Generations," *Wall Street Journal* (updated November 20, 2015), www.wsj.com/articles/how-to-keep-a-family-business-alive-for-generations-1444 8045760. Retrieved October 4, 2016.
5. James E. Hughes Jr., Susan E. Massenzio, and Keith Whitaker, *The Voice of the Rising Generation* (Hoboken, NJ: John Wiley & Sons, 2014), pp. 14–17.
6. Ibid.
7. "The 25 Best Practices of Multi-Generational Families, www.genspring.com/ . . . / 25-best-practices-of-multi-generational-families," *GenSpring* (December 16, 2014). Retrieved February 20, 2016.
8. Pat McNees, http://www.patmcnees.com/what_is_an_ethical_will___a_legacy _letter_44837.htm. Retrieved September 29, 2016.

CHAPTER 7

Vision and Mission: The Past, the Present, and the Future

When an individual or a family accumulates resources that are enough to survive the wealth creator, they are transformed from wealth consumers to wealth stewards. In this role, they assume the added responsibility of making decisions that could affect multiple family members and generations far into the future. They begin to understand and appreciate both the responsibility and the opportunity they have to influence current family members and future generations in a positive or negative way. They see the need to take a strategic approach to planning for today's generations and those who will follow them.

As new households are added, the family begins to resemble not only a typical ancestral tree but also an *organization* whose members are related by blood or marriage. To keep the fortune and family intact, a formal structure that allows for joint decision making and conflict resolution becomes more important.

The Family Office Exchange coined the term *instividual*, which brings together the concept of family members connected as an organization through their common ownership of wealth. At this point, the family takes on many of the characteristics of a business, including a leadership group, those in control of the wealth; a stakeholder or stockholder group, those with a current or future ownership stake; and often an employee group, those who work for the family to help manage the shared resources.

The Essential Question

Before a family begins its journey into all the activities surrounding the management of wealth as a group, members must ask themselves a critical question: Are we a family or are we simply people related to the same antecedents?[1] From that question come many more:

- Do we have similar values that could form the basis for a coherent wealth management strategy?
- Do those values come from a sense of shared family heritage and history?
- Are we willing to work together for the benefit of the family as an entity, even if it means giving up some of our own autonomy?
- Do we trust one another, or are there deep divisions within the family that would make it difficult or unpleasant to work as a family unit?
- If we have never considered these critical questions, are we willing to examine them now? Will we be happy to take the time and make the effort required to set the stage for understanding one another and making decisions together so that all may prosper?

If the answers to these questions suggest a willingness and an ability to pull all the oars in the same direction at the same time, it may be time to build the family boat.

Christian Caspar, Ana Karina Dias, and Heinz-Peter Elstrodt[2] mention that family businesses that endure do so because they are well-run and governed by agreements that are written down and understood by those family members who are part of the business. They go on to say that "the interpretation of these agreements, and the governance decisions guided by them, may involve several kinds of family forums. A family council representing different branches and generations of the family, for instance, may be responsible to a larger family assembly used to build consensus on major issues."

For families of shared wealth who have agreed that common wealth management is a sensible course, the most useful way to build a decision-making framework is to establish a set of organizational or governance tools, including a vision statement, mission statement, and family constitution and bylaws. These tools help the family keep in tune, clarify the roles of each group of stakeholders, and share the beliefs of the wealth owners with current and future generations. They also provide a defined exit strategy for any stakeholder who does not agree with the principles and structure and therefore chooses to leave.

The best way to bring these useful tools to fruition is for the family to craft them with the help of an experienced facilitator. By creating these foundational documents, the family builds the platform on which to set a solid and sustainable family wealth management structure. The vision and mission statements articulate the individual and shared values of the current group of family members. These values represent the family's fundamental beliefs and are the driving factors for decision making in their day-to-day lives. They are created by past experiences and learnings and they form the foundation of what the family believes will be important in the future. Understanding and memorializing the family's past experiences, present values, and vision for the future provides a common purpose around which to align the family and its wealth. This common purpose allows them to create goals and objectives concerning how they manage their wealth.

In many families, the need for new goals becomes apparent when the family sells a closely held business they shared as owners or future owners. For a protracted period of time, the family business may have served as a rallying point around which family members gathered and bonded, told stories, and imparted values. However, if the business is sold, the focal point of the family organization disappears. The family is no longer a business-owing family but a financial family. As the Hawthorn Institute puts it, "A business owner family is ... a single family that exercises control over a closely held business. A financial family is ... a multigenerational family that has attained affluence primarily through the successful operation and sale of a closely held family business."[3]

After the sale, the family may be very wealthy, but it often lacks the unity the organization of the business provided for it. At this juncture, family members come face to face with the challenges of shared ownership outside the family business and the importance of the structure and fellowship the business offered. The idea of applying family business principles to the new business of family becomes attractive as the group reaches for coherence, effective decision making, and efficiency in managing their new circumstances.

Vision and Mission

Although they are related, a vision statement and a mission statement are not the same things. The Foundation Center defines the two: "A vision statement expresses an organization's optimal goal and reason for existence, while a mission statement provides an overview of the group's plans to realize that vision by identifying the service areas, target audience, and values and goals of the organization."[4]

A vision statement defines what the family believes is the optimal way of being in the world and offers inspiration and guidance as family members work toward that goal. It's aspirational and a touchstone for the family when they are making crucial decisions about who they are and what they support. The statement should be memorable and easy for everyone to understand. It might serve as the opening of any family meeting, so it is reinforced for adults' understanding and children's learning.

A vision statement looks to the future. It's a "we will" promise, although many organizations don't use that exact wording. CVS, for example, wants to "improve the quality of human life."[5] And at Ford Motor Company, the vision is "people working together as a lean, global enterprise to make people's lives better through automotive and mobility leadership."[6]

Like businesses, private foundations have their own visions that are based on a variety of factors. For example, the vision of the Samuel Bronfman Foundation is to "inspire the Jewish community to leave this world a better place than we found it," and the W. K. Kellogg Foundation envisions "a nation that marshals its resources to assure that all children have an equitable and promising future—a nation in which all children thrive."

A mission statement is somewhat more pragmatic and practical. As Andrew Bangser, president of Foundation Source, said, "An effective mission is one you have the scale to accomplish. Biting off the right size chunk of the problem is the key in being able to make a difference."[7]

The creation of a vision statement helps the family stay on track even in the face of difficulties such as the death of a family member who has had a significant role in leading the organization. A clearly defined vision keeps the ship afloat even as the waves are rising.

A mission statement, on the other hand, has a shorter time frame and can be adapted to meet changing circumstances. In an article for *Psychology Today*, Janelle Evans says that a mission statement "defines the present state or purpose of an organization ... and answers three questions about why an organization exists:

- What it does
- Who it does it for
- How it does what it does"[8]

The American Red Cross mission statement covers all the *who, what,* and *how* bases with its mission statement, which says the organization "prevents and alleviates human suffering in the face of emergencies by mobilizing the power of volunteers and the generosity of donors."[9]

The St. Jude Children's Research Hospital has a strong mission statement: "... to advance cures, and means of prevention, for pediatric catastrophic diseases through research and treatment. Consistent with the vision of our founder Danny Thomas, no child is denied treatment based on race, religion or a family's ability to pay." Donations pour into the hospital to help make that promise a reality.[10]

At the MacArthur Foundation, a massive private foundation, the mission involves creating a "more just, verdant, and peaceful world,"[11] and the foundation has the resources to make a major difference in the areas they support. These wide-ranging interests include health, population, education, conservation, arts, and culture to name just a few.

In 1953, the Howard Hughes Medical Foundation stated that "the primary purpose and objective of the Howard Hughes Medical Institute shall be the promotion of human knowledge within the field of the basic sciences (principally the field of medical research and medical education) and the effective application thereof for the benefit of mankind."[12] Even a cursory look at the statement provides a clear picture of what the foundation will support and how it will do it.

The Ford Foundation mission says, in part, "Across eight decades, our mission has been to reduce poverty and injustice, strengthen democratic values, promote international cooperation, and advance human achievement."

Although not stated as a mission, The Lilly Endowment says it "exists to support the causes of religion, education, and community development. The Endowment affords special emphasis to projects that benefit young people and promote leadership education and financial self-sufficiency in the nonprofit, charitable sector."[13] Although the endowment awards grants elsewhere, the organization notes that its primary interests are in the city of Indianapolis, where the Eli Lilly corporate offices are located, and the state of Indiana.

Families seeking to create their own mission statements may put more emphasis on one of the three traits Evans mentions, and the language of the statement may be revised as it is reviewed periodically based on economic conditions or new priorities and possibilities. Although it can be revamped, revision should not take place unilaterally. Like a vision statement, the mission statement looks forward with optimism, but it is oriented toward action rather than contemplation.

A mission statement, like an ethical will, is not a legal document, but it is a useful guide for making important decisions, enhancing family harmony, and ameliorating conflicts that might never have surfaced had great wealth not entered the picture. Money can bring out the best in a family, but if it's not managed well, it also can open up old wounds and result in anger, frustration, and hostility.

Creating a vision or mission statement takes more planning than simply sitting around in a living room with a bunch of family members and having everyone shout out what they believe in. Discussions like this can become circular, contentious, and unproductive if they are not well structured. A trained facilitator skilled in consensus building can be helpful in leading the exercise. The facilitator can capture and categorize input, assist the family in recognizing where commonalities exist even in areas of disagreement, keep the discussion moving by periodically restating the essence of the exercise, and, most important, make sure the process isn't dictated solely by the wealth creator or a small cabal of older family members.

Vision or mission statements that are imposed rather than agreed to are statements that will fail. Family members who have no input will be resentful and disinclined to participate in making the family mission work. They may not be actively hostile, but they will be far less committed to the success of the process.

Getting Started

To create the vision statement, it helps to look once again at the family's history and consider what insights or guiding principles suggest the foundational values. Writing a vision statement can take several hours or even a few days; once again, it's helpful to employ a professional and objective facilitator to manage the meeting. Prior to organizing the family session, a survey or questionnaire could be administered to the adult family members, both to gain their feedback and to motivate their participation in the meeting. The questions in such a survey often involve family dynamics and how to come to a mutual understanding around values. They might look something like this:

In your opinion:

- What are the values that most bind us as a family? How do we enact them? How do we instill them in the next generations?
- What have we discovered to be the strengths of the family? Are there traits and tendencies that undermine our strengths? How do we deal with them now? How *should* we deal with them?
- What are the roadblocks to family unity? What can we do to remove them?
- How do we choose the family leaders? By age/generation, skills and talents, or some other qualification?
- How do we deal with inevitable changes such as death?
- How do we take care of one another if or when we become unable to carry out our responsibilities?
- What do we do if we have serious disagreements about decisions that are being made by the family leadership?
- How should the youngest generation be educated about the family's legacy? At what age should that begin? When should this generation become part of the decision-making processes?

The Values Edge System: An Exercise in Personal and Team Discovery, which "clarifies personal values, enhances relationships, [and] strengthens team performance,"[14] is sometimes a very effective tool to help structure the discussion and align the input of the key family stakeholders. This system, created by Dr. Dennis Jaffe and Dr. Cynthia Scott, offers a mechanism by which family members can understand and communicate their individual and shared values. The system originally was designed to foster organizational effectiveness for management teams and employees of operating businesses. However, given the similarities of the issues families of wealth face in working together, this system also can serve the purpose of bringing the family into agreement with a communal set of values. Other types of instruments also may work for specific families.

Once family members understand and document their independent and shared values, they can use the areas of commonality to develop the basis for a vision statement. For example, say a particular family identifies the following five values as the ones that collectively are most meaningful to the family:

1. Spirituality
2. Family harmony
3. Community
4. Integrity
5. Health

A subset of family members might then work together to write two or three options using the five values for the family to vote on. The options might include:

- With our family's foundation in our reverence for God, we will encourage family members to live physically and socially healthy lives with a focus on integrity. We will use our resources to inspire family harmony and support for the communities we live and work in.
- Spirituality is at the core of who we are as a family and is the guidepost for how we will live our lives, with integrity and a focus on family unity, healthy living, and our greater community.
- The health of the community is our highest value, and we will dedicate a portion of the family wealth to supporting programs that promote physical, emotional, and social well-being.

From questioning, participating, and, most important, listening to each other, a family often will be able to discern a vision that supports its shared history and values. Because of its long strategic view, the vision statement usually remains a constant North Star over the years.

Of course, the resulting document is important, but the process itself is equally so. Working together on a concentrated project can help resolve old conflicts, reveal unexpected talents, and tease out new directions the family might wish to explore. Creating the document can be exciting and energizing for every member of the family.

Once the family has been successful in defining its vision, it can move on to the mission statement: the document that defines how the family will act out its vision. As before, questions can be the catalyst to get the family talking and agreeing. Inquiries around mission tend to deal more with shorter term, day-to-day decisions and might include such topics as:

- How should we *use* our financial and human resources to support our family vision?
- How should we *invest* our money to make it support the family's values for generations?
- What are the activities and opportunities we should consider and encourage to strengthen the family?
- What should we avoid and discourage among family members?

Because of its shorter term, the mission statement is somewhat more fluid and tactical. A mission statement needn't be lengthy; a paragraph or two may suffice. If we use the first hypothetical vision statement from the prior example, the mission statement might be:

The mission for our family is:

- To encourage family investments and activities that are congruent with our spiritual values.
- To inspire, support, and resource healthy lifestyles in the community and to help family members and others who are struggling with health issues.
- To work and play together as a family by providing consistent and compelling opportunities to interact and participate while encouraging and supporting individuality.
- To accept our responsibility as part of larger society and use a significant portion of our time, money, and talent to support the greater good and to monitor and measure the results.

Families with Purpose suggests a three-pronged approach to writing the statement: action, the manner in which the action is carried out, and the benefits or results of the action.[15] The following examples show this principle in practice:

- As a united family, to care for one another and participate in impact investment in the technologies and ideas that will provide better lives for the members of our community, city, and state.

- To increase our family fortune by following the ethical precepts of those who came before us and to ensure the finest education and the widest array of vocational choices for those who follow us.
- To improve the health and economy of the world by using a significant portion of our shared resources to support cutting-edge research in the treatment and elimination of Alzheimer's disease, which devastates families and may cause international economic chaos within the next thirty years.
- To work with other families of means to identify areas of emerging global concern and to partner with international organizations to devise solutions that will result in stronger, healthier societies throughout the world.

It's evident that family mission statements are as different as the families themselves. However, no matter how the family defines its values, vision, and mission, the written documents are invaluable in creating family fellowship and movement toward a united and thriving future.

Notes

1. This question is based on the work of Lisa Gray, *Generational Wealth Management* (London: Euromoney Trading, Ltd., 2010).
2. Christian Caspar, Ana Karina Dias, and Heinz-Peter Elstrodt, "The Five Attributes of Enduring Family Businesses," McKinsey and Company (January 2010), www.mckinsey.com/business-functions/organization/our-insights/the-five-attributes-of-enduring-family-businesses. Retrieved April 30, 2016.
3. Hawthorn Institute, "Transferring the Seven Principles of a Successful Family Business," www.pnc.com/content/dam/pnc-com/pdf/personal/Hawthorn_PNC _Family_Wealth/Hawthorn%20Institute_7%20Principles_1215.pdf. Retrieved April 27, 2016.
4. foundationcenter.org/getstarted/tutorials/establish/statements.html. Retrieved April 29, 2016.
5. CVS website, cvs.com.
6. Ford Motor Company website, corporate.ford.com/company.html. Retrieved April 30, 2016.
7. Nancy Opiela, "Seven Tips for a Successful Family Foundation," *Advisor Perspectives* (March 30, 2010), www.advisorperspectives.com/newsletters10/pdfs/Seven _Tips_for_a_Successful_Family_Foundation.pdf. Retrieved August 24, 2016.
8. Jannell Evans, "Vision and Mission: What's the Difference and Why Does It Matter?" *Psychology Today* (April 10, 2010). Retrieved April 29, 2016.
9. American Red Cross website, www.redcross.org. Retrieved April 29, 2016.
10. St. Jude Children's Research Hospital website, www.stjude.org/about-st-jude .html.
11. MacArthur Foundation website, www.macfound.org/about/.
12. Howard Hughes Medical Institute website, www.hhmi.org/about/history.
13. Lilly Endowment, Inc. website, www.lillyendowment.org/theendowment.html.
14. "The Values Edge: Defining Personal and Family Values." http://www.dennis jaffe.com/.
15. Family Mission Statement, www.familieswithpurpose.com/family-mission-statement/. Retrieved April 28, 2016.

CHAPTER 8

Family Governance: Roles and Responsibilities, Decision Making, and Conflict Resolution

Creating wealth is somewhat like building a fleet of sailboats. When wealth creators first set out, it's typical for them to buy and paint the boat, provision it, scrape the hull, hoist the sails, and keep a firm hand on the tiller, all the while scanning the horizon for dicey weather. As they succeed and add to their flotillas, it becomes necessary for them to bring on more hands, yet the creators continue to make decisions about each boat. At some point, however, it's possible that every boat is taking on water, and the founder of the fleet is unable to plug all the holes. Now it's time for the redistribution of responsibilities. The creator is still heavily involved, but others are assuming duties in which they have particular expertise.

As a family business expands, especially into the second generation, the wealth creator still tends to make major decisions on behalf of the family while he or she is in good health and able to do so. This centralization of power and control is natural and based on the founder's role in establishing the family's wealth. The wealth creator defines other family members' rights and responsibilities, even as the family grows in shared wealth and the number of people who have an ownership interest. The wealth creator may informally delegate some responsibilities, but as the wealth grows, so do the risks in neglecting to put structure into the roles and responsibilities for each family.

If informality rules the family enterprise, the risks include a faulty succession plan, poor decision making, and confusion about a number of factors.

A less-than-adequate succession plan will hamper and may even destroy the business itself. A recent PWC survey covering 2,400 business decision makers in more than forty countries found that only 16 percent had an agreed-upon and written succession plan in place, although more than 80 percent had conflict resolution procedures in place.[1] It stands to reason, however, that conflict can best be avoided by having the succession plan drawn up, talked about, and accepted by the business and the family. Resolving issues up front is far better than trying to tie up a tangle of loose ends after the retirement, incapacity, or death of the founder.

Decisions are affected by communication, and poor communication can result in bad decisions. Without a well-defined communication process, the conversations between and among family members who are active in the business and those who are not, between family members and nonfamily employees, and between generations of the family can resemble the old game of Telephone; that is, the messages may be garbled, incomplete, and tinged with self-interest. That's a blueprint for slipshod decision making.

For example, family members who work in the business are more conversant with information as it becomes available simply because of their positions in daily operations. Those who are owners but not employees typically must wait for information to trickle down, perhaps by attending a family meeting or reading a quarterly email. They may feel excluded and as if they are second-class members of the family, which can lead to disharmony and alienation.

In addition, they may be more deliberate in processing the data and making decisions simply because they are removed from the day-to-day life of the family business. This perceived slowness can be irritating to the family members in the business, who want to make choices quickly and efficiently.

If not addressed in advance, these issues will become harder to resolve as the wealth creator reduces his or her role in the oversight of the family business or wealth management.

Instituting Family Governance

Each family member has one or more roles with regard to the assets held in common. These positions can include owner, employee, manager, board or committee member, leader, trustee, or beneficiary. Each role has varying levels of rights, accountabilities, and responsibilities, and sometimes the roles conflict. For example, if those who work in the family business see expansion as a primary value, the board of directors may take action to enhance that value by acquiring a competitor.

However, those who are not part of the business but count on income from its operations may be surprised, chagrined, or even horrified or furious to hear that their portion of the wealth will be reduced or not disbursed at all for a twelve-month period because of the costs related to the acquisition. If the facts have not been communicated adequately, a rift is in the making. A systemized structure becomes necessary to balance interests and rights. The best way to organize these functions is by devising some form of family governance.

Governing the Family

The term *family governance* can sound off-putting, rigid, bureaucratic, and even a little pretentious. However, the purpose of family governance is to create an organizational structure that encompasses the family's vision and mission, roles and rights, and provides the necessary guidelines and tools to manage the shared resources most effectively. It allows for centralized decision making while offering both transparency and accountability to every member of the family. As Lisa Gray says, "Effective governance is a set of processes and systems which have been carefully designed by leadership based on input from the family and voluntarily adopted by all family members to ... serve the family and to protect [and] foster the family's authentic wealth."[2]

Optimal family governance:

- Treats the family members like a family and the family enterprise like a business.
- Recognizes crossovers between the family and the enterprise.
- Establishes clear boundaries among governance constituents.
- Identifies and honors the differences, goals, and objectives of individual family members.
- Acknowledges and manages family and wealth dynamics.
- Develops the family's human, intellectual, and social capital.
- Allows members to earn a voice in business governance by evidencing qualifications that convey the right to be heard.

Families are complicated entities, and different members have various needs, some of which are illustrated in the following table:

Family	Owners	Managers
Communication	Communication	Communication
Strong relationships	Appreciation and cash distributions	Clear direction from owners
Responsible, empowered individuals	Financial reports and information	Understanding of long-term strategic vision
Education and development opportunities	Nonfinancial business information	Opportunity to create and implement plans to meet strategic vision
Family and business reputation	Information about strategic plans; business reputation	Compensation that is competitive and rewarding
Sense of family, values, and history	Community legacy	Appreciation for achievement
Understanding of potential roles, both inside and outside the business	Long-term exit/legacy plans	Opportunities for advancement
Nonfinancial business information	Opportunity to help shape legacy	Independence; respect for boundaries
Retirement benefits for former employees	Retirement benefits for former employees	Retirement benefits for former employees

Given these various and sometimes divergent needs, governance brings clarity. Without a governance structure, extended families that are growing sometimes fall into the trap of slap-dash functioning. The decision-making processes may become haphazard, even sloppy, and this lack of order can result in missed opportunities, poor communication, and great frustration among family members, owners, and managers. That confusion can ultimately lead to hostility and family breakdown.

Sometimes, families don't understand their need for governance until a crisis occurs and they must scurry about, trying to jerry-rig some sort of plan out of parts and pieces. When that doesn't work well—or at all—they get down to the business of creating a process and putting it into action. Within the governance framework, the family operates more efficiently and effectively as an organization. With a guiding plan in place, they can make decisions more quickly, seize wealth-enhancing opportunities, and devise clear expectations of themselves and others, all of which greatly reduces the risk of conflict.

Governance can include a family constitution, bylaws, boards, employment and investment policies, and expectations around family meetings and reporting of information. Whatever structures are put in place, the constitution makes it easier for family members to understand their places and functions within the wealth enterprise.

The Family Constitution and Bylaws

This important document also can be called a family creed, protocol, or charter, but whatever the term, the constitution sets out the family's commitment to the vision and mission statements they previously drafted and to the roles and responsibilities family members will assume, either within the family business or in managing the assets if a liquidity event has resulted in sudden wealth for the family as a whole. Administratively, it articulates how the vision and values will play out in the daily life of the family—for example, how they will make investment decisions, choose new initiatives to support, or develop their philanthropic outreach, to mention only a few. The constitution may do the following:

• Formalize the family's values.
• Establish conflict management, decision making, and communication protocols.
• Define the purpose and rules for each governance body.
• Outline continuity and succession plans.
• Create checks and balances to manage competing interests.
• Define individual family member rights and obligations.
• Regulate common interests to work toward predictable and fair treatment.
• Encourage individual accountability.
• Create a framework for changes.

The bylaws to the family constitution highlight *how* the constitution will function. They govern the powers, duties, and rights of directors and management, as well as the procedures and rules for shareholder meetings and voting rights. They also set up the communication channels and establish procedures for conflict resolution within the business and family.

Families are unique, and family constitutions should reflect that uniqueness. Although a template constitution may be useful in discussing the issues that surround the creation of the actual document, the constitution itself should not be something ripped out of a book and applied wholesale to decisions as important as these. No template can take into account the family dynamics—that is, the myriad feelings and interests of a wide-ranging, multiple-unit family.

Drafting the constitution should not be delegated solely to the advisors or family office, either. They may be skilled at what they do, but not have the vision to anticipate or mediate the types of intrafamily conflicts that sometimes arise when the topics are money and fairness. Of course, the advisors should be invited to contribute their expertise, professional insights, and support to the process, but the hard work of crafting the constitution falls to the family. It is in that hard work that the family forges its identity and builds its unity. In fact, the documents—the vision and mission statement and the constitution and bylaws—while important, are not really the point. The effort is. "Without the hard work required to educate the family members and to enable them to offer valuable, thoughtful input, any seeming benefit gained by the creation of these documents may be short-lived."[3]

The constitution consolidates into one entity all those who deal with the family wealth: the family itself, the family office if one exists, representatives of wealth advisory and legal firms, and individual advisors, if any, so that everyone works together cohesively in the family's interests. By putting everyone on the same page, rather than at cross-purposes, it often is possible for the family to sidestep the types of disputes and disruptions that destroy harmony and consensus.

The family constitution can govern nearly any eventuality the family wishes to consider: succession planning if the business is still owned by the family or considerations about if and when the business should be sold; how responsibilities will be divided; and how the next generation will be selected and educated for leadership roles. It also can cover potentially difficult situations such as death or disability of a key member or the divorce, remarriage, and subsequent change in family structure (through the addition of stepchildren) of any member.

Most important to the success of the constitution may be the portions dealing with the resolution of disputes among family members. Not all families are well-attuned to one another, and if bad blood exists in the first generation, the animosity may rear its head again in subsequent generations, causing discord among brothers, sisters, and cousins. However, if the family can work through disagreements by themselves according to the provisions of the family constitution, it may be possible for them to avoid ugly, public litigation.

It's vital that the family constitution be a written document. Memory is fallible and subject to bias, so having everything that has been agreed upon committed to paper or other media prevents useless, petty debates that gum up the efficiency of the family enterprise.

Working on something of value to everyone can bring family members closer, even if they are scattered across the country and have come together only for this purpose. Because sharing is crucial to the success of the endeavor, cousins who barely know one another may find they have much in common and become excited about being the next generation to act out the family compact.

Intergenerational conversations can bring new ideas to the fore, and the older family members may be energized by the younger and be more willing to pass the torch at the appropriate time. Because everyone is encouraged to be part of the discussion, trust is built even if the interchanges are sometimes heated.

The conversations leading to the final documents may not be all peaches and cream. Some things are hard to think about, let alone raise publicly. It may make attendees nervous to talk about what happens after the death of the wealth creator if he or she is sitting in the room with the rest of the clan. It's unpleasant to consider which family members might need someone else to manage their affairs in the event that their aging brings incapacity. It can be touchy to talk about the care requirements of a child with special needs or to consider what to do about the uncle with the substance abuse problem. Nearly every family has these kinds of "third-rail" predicaments, and often it's best to once again call upon a specially trained facilitator who can help dial back the emotion and keep the conversation moving.

Whatever the family circumstances might be, agreements based on openness, honesty, cooperation, and compromise, all wrapped around the core of family values, vision, and mission, give the family legacy a much greater chance of survival from generation to generation than if the process is left to chance and casual conversation.

Changing the Constitution

Although based on a family's unchangeable truths, the family constitution is a living document that can be amended as conditions change. For example, if the family drew up the constitution while still involved in a family business, the document probably will need considerable alteration if the business is sold and wealth pours in.

Once the organizational/family structure provided by the business disappears, the family constitution may become the tent pole around which the family gathers, so it's important that the document be up to date and reflective of where the group is now. At one time, the major constitutional issues might have included such topics as the conditions under which family members were to be hired by the business, but if the business is gone, the new focus might be on how to invest and use the wealth gained by the sale so the family legacy is best perpetuated.

Additionally, as generations rise and fall and life conditions change, what was important to the wealth creators 100 years ago may be far less so to their successors. Although the values the family members have articulated tend to remain constant, the ways in which they enact those values may shift. At that point, some aspects of the constitution may be revisited and altered to reflect the times in which the family finds itself.

However, even though an amendment policy is part of the constitution, the founding document never should be amended on a whim or because one family member suddenly becomes huffy about a particular bone of contention. Amendments are generally to be reserved for substantive items about which the majority of the family members are in agreement.

It's Not All about Rights

While a constitution often is concerned with the rights of those who are governed by it, it's also useful to enumerate the responsibilities that attend the rights. For example, with the right of having a vote at family meetings comes the responsibility to attend as many of them as possible and to be prepared to participate by reading documents and policies sent in advance of the gathering. With the right to be considered for a leadership role within the family comes the responsibility to work constructively and cooperatively with other members of the group. With the right to be compensated for work done in behalf of the family comes the responsibility not to shirk the duties and to keep on top of opportunities that will benefit all and ensure the increase of the family wealth and the continuation of the legacy.

The Family Assembly and the Family Council

The writing of the constitution generally includes a provision for ways in which the family conducts its daily interactions. The family assembly and family council are two such methods.

The family assembly is a forum to which all family members are invited to discuss business and family issues. During the founder's stage of the business, the family assembly may take the form of an informal family meeting, which, like the first-generation Rockefellers' philanthropic discussions, may take place around the breakfast table. The duties of the family assembly include:

- Approval of any change in the family values and vision
- Education of family members about their rights and responsibilities
- Approval of family employment and compensation policies
- Election of family council members (if a council exists)
- Election of other family committees' members
- Other important family matters

As the family expands, these meetings usually become more formal in nature and allow the members to communicate values, generate new business ideas, and prepare the next generation of the family business leaders. If the business has passed out of the family's hands, the family assembly still may continue to meet to learn about external influences such as changes to the tax code and macroeconomic conditions that might affect the family's wealth management plans. There may be discussion about investment strategies or philanthropic options.

Some family meetings may feature presentations on subjects such as conflict resolution or preparing children to become good stewards of money and other resources. In short, well-orchestrated family meetings lasting a couple of days can cover a range of topics and be of great value to attendees.

However, between these all-hands meetings, decisions must be made and actions taken to keep the family moving in the direction set by the constitution and bylaws. When families become too large and unwieldy to manage these tasks, they may designate a group of family members to deal with issues and opportunities requiring quick responses. This group—the family council—helps to interpret the foundational documents and carries out other duties that arise in managing a large, complex, multigenerational unit.

The underlying purpose of the council is to promote a sense of cohesiveness and unity across generations while also developing the family's policies, direction, human capital, and intellectual capital in an effort to create a sense of accountability, stewardship, and leadership.

The council is the primary link between the family, the board, and senior management of the business. Some of their duties include the following:

- Suggesting and discussing names of candidates for board membership.
- Providing the enterprise's board with the owners' strategic plans and needs (financial and otherwise).
- Drafting and revising family position papers on its vision, mission, and values.

- Drafting and revising family policies such as family employment, compensation, and family shareholding policies.
- Dealing with other important matters to the family, including philanthropic ventures and financial concerns.

They also may be responsible for establishing and communicating important family policies regarding decision making, confidentiality, conduct, risk management (including insurance coverages, estate planning, prenuptial agreements, and traditional and social media policies), and communication planning.

In short, the council is a busy working group that handles day-to-day details; speaks with the advisors; communicates with the larger group of relatives; and acts as the canary in the coal mine, sensing potential conflicts and helping to defuse them before they become battlegrounds.

The makeup of the family council probably is contained in the constitution and is the result of careful consideration of a variety of questions, including:

- Who may serve on the council? Lineal descendants only or in-laws? May younger generations be considered for service when they reach legal majority, or will some other qualification be required, such as a certain number of years of increasing responsibility in the family business or outside employment? What types of experience are considered essential for participation?
- Will decisions be made by consensus? Those who have worked in consensus organizations mention that consensus decision making is time-consuming and often laborious, but that the process usually results in better buy-in because every member has found something in the decision he or she can support. Rancor is less likely to erupt.
- If one member of the council is representing more branches of the family than another member, does the larger bloc always have more clout than the smaller? Do senior members of the family have more voting power than the younger members? Or does the one-person-one-vote rule pertain, no matter what the age or length of company service?

Generally, the council includes representatives of each branch of the family and several generations, but how they are selected and the roles they fill are determined by individual families. Terms of office are prescribed and duties are carefully laid out.

It goes without saying that those who serve on the family council must be loyal, faithful stewards of the family's assets and legacy. Their duties may be comprehensive (based largely on whether the family is still active in the family business), but almost always include:

- Being the keepers of the family values and mission and certifying that decisions are in keeping with what the family has accepted as its guiding principles.
- Keeping the family informed—and providing documentation—about decisions that have been or will be taken.
- Ensuring that those who are part of the council are adequately trained for their roles and that the next generation is appropriately educated about the duties they will assume at the appropriate time.
- Setting the agenda for the family meetings, selecting a venue, and managing or delegating the details of activities other than the meeting itself (e.g., a family dinner, a theater excursion, a ziplining adventure, or a day camp experience for youngsters who will not be attending the meeting itself).

Of course, if the family is still engaged in its primary business, members of the family council have a major role to play in communication between the family and the board of directors and management.

Those in positions of authority in the family council must be strong, vigorous leaders, but not iron-fisted dictators. Their job is to assist the family in making the best decisions about their wealth and legacy, to listen carefully, to answer questions, and to lead and participate willingly in discussion, not to impose their will on the rest of the family.

Types of Governance

As has been indicated in several of this book's earlier case studies, the patriarchal style of top-down governance, implemented solely by the wealth creator and perhaps a few trusted advisors, almost never succeeds. Why would it? Family members have little voice, feel disrespected, and have no particular desire to participate in a structure that doesn't allow for real engagement. They don't learn much about the family business because decisions are made by the wealth creator with only token input from other members of the family. Family members often throw up their hands and disengage completely from both the rest of the family and the family business. Disengagement can lead to disaster as the family struggles to uphold its stated values and mission in the face of authoritarian management.

Lisa Gray mentions other ways that families may choose to govern themselves: majority rule, for one, in which each family member has a vote. She indicates that this style may appear to be most fair, but may fall prey to factionalism, as family members form cliques who vote together, leaving the minority members feeling excluded. As Gray says, "Pure democracies with no checks and balances can breed anarchy; a flat governance structure ruled by majority vote can have the same effect in families."[4]

Gray appears to favor the representative democracy model, saying, "[This form] ... that has checks and balances of authority is effective for current generations and also offers the greatest flexibility to accommodate transitions the family experiences from generation to generation."[5]

Indeed, this last form of governance seems to be the one most recommended by those who deal with families with significant resources and results in the formation of family assemblies and councils that hear the voices of the family and represent those voices in decision making.

A Critical Factor

No matter how carefully a family plans its operations and writes its policies, if the deliberations and decision are not well-communicated, the door is left open for misunderstandings that can result in discord. A good communication plan should do the following:

- Promote a sense of belonging, inclusiveness, and unity.
- Provide frequent, timely, relevant information to all stakeholders.
- Generate awareness and excitement about the directions and actions the family is taking.
- Disseminate both good and bad news.
- Examine contentious issues while attempting to limit conflict among stakeholders.
- Share concerns and achievements.
- Educate family members and invite input.

The plan should incorporate a variety of communication methods, including a family email group or website, newsletters, surveys, conference calls, meetings, educational opportunities and workshops, and voting or proxy materials. All these outreach activities are useful in encouraging input from every family member who wishes to participate. Older members may prefer print communications while younger ones almost always wish to receive information electronically.

Insofar as possible, communication among family members should be judgment free, which can be a hard standard to adhere to when several generations are involved. With today's longer life spans, even a relatively small family can have three or four generations with widely varying worldviews represented at family meetings. Sometimes these divergent family representatives can come to surprising consensus around specific issues. For example, both traditionalists (those who probably created the family wealth and still may be very robust and active in their seventies and eighties) and Millennials (those between the ages of eighteen and thirty-three) believe in harnessing the power of teamwork.

On the other hand, traditionalists have respect for leaders while Millennials are more likely to demand that leaders respect *them* and their ideas. For traditionalists, frequent job change might have been viewed as instability, while Millennials expect to change jobs—and entire careers—several times during their lives.

Older wealth creators may have viewed long hours in the office as dues to be paid for advancement, reward, and a place at the table. Younger family members, however, may feel they are at work 24 hours a day because their constant use of communications devices keeps them in touch wherever they are. They may see a traditional office environment as a confining space that saps creativity. They think they should be rewarded for the quality of their work, not the quantity of time they've spent in the office. With all the technology they have at their fingertips, they believe they can answer a question or solve a problem while watching their kids' soccer games just as easily as they can sitting at a desk in a cubicle farm. A balanced life is far more important to them than it was to earlier generations.

Generational differences regarding the nature of work, life balance, tolerance for risk, and a variety of other factors can make family communication difficult. Although these differences are simply alternative ways of looking at the same set of facts, if family members see them as misguided, antiquated, selfish, entitled, or just plain wrong, and the language between generations reflects these biases, the stage is set for disputes and unnecessary arguments. Families threatened with fracture should seek refuge in their common values and look for areas of agreement and perhaps some professional facilitation.

The most powerful governance models give voice and some sort of voting participation to every member of the family except children. The adults' voices are heard at family assemblies, and their votes may elect the family council or other advisory bodies and may be sought on matters of policy and procedures. While the model may not be a pure democracy with each family member voting on every single issue, the representative style prescribed by many family constitutions, combined with a strong communication plan, can make every family member feel heard and included.

It is the number-one responsibility of every family member to be committed to the vision and mission statements, the family constitution, and all other documents that underlie the family's future and legacy. As John

Ward, PhD, said, "An ownership group that speaks with one voice liberates management to focus on the business.... Responsibility includes respecting the limits of ownership's roles, understanding the business and providing leadership for the governance process."[6] This is equally true if a liquidity event has occurred and the family has made the transition from family-owned business to financial family. At that point, there must be coherence in policies and procedures that "create[s] a sense of mutual purpose ... in managing the areas that remain."[7]

James Hughes mentioned that "the ability of siblings and cousins to work together is critical to long-term wealth preservation."[8] It's reasonable to assume, then, that these siblings and cousins must be consistently exposed to the guiding documents and be part of extensive conversations over time that clearly articulate the family's values and planning for the future. "If any generation fails to reaffirm ... the family's social compact, the ability of later generations to resurrect [it] will ... be greatly diminished,"[9] Hughes added.

Right from the beginning and throughout generational shifts, the foundational documents should be set alongside real-world behavior to see if the family is continuing to act in a way that reflects what it started out to do. Although times and attitudes change, the values should be immutable, and if the family is not living up to its own mission, it's time for someone—possibly the family council—to pull on the reins and redirect the rest of the clan. If the family adheres to the agreed-upon of values during a particular set of circumstances but abandons them in the face of difficulties or unexpected events, discord is almost a given, and the family legacy may be on its last legs.

When Conflict Threatens the Family Enterprise

As we've seen in the stories of well-known families and in the case studies in this book, even the best preparation may not be enough to forestall disagreements, so often protracted and bitter. Before family members haul one another into court, however, there may be another way to resolve or even prevent family disintegration.

Anchorage, Alaska, judge magistrate Suzanne Cole shares the following insight on the *importance of problem solving*:

> "Most people agree that unless it's absolutely necessary, litigation is rarely the best option for family disputes. Some form of alternative dispute resolution is preferable. At times, a professional mediator or arbitrator may be appropriate. However, I always encourage family members to use

the principles of mediation in their family meetings or to resolve inter- or intra-family disagreements—and to avoid the 'take no prisoners' animosity that can develop when issues simmer and remain unresolved for too long. It is far more effective to address anticipated concerns or areas of potential disagreement than to wait until they have ripened into full-blown and entrenched disputes.

"Conflict is inevitable. It can even be positive. It can be argued that conflict is a necessary ingredient for growth within individuals, families, and communities. If disputes are left to bubble without an effective means of addressing them, most systems, including families, will boil over. A system is only as strong as its ability to resolve conflicts with integrity, while preserving the well-being of its members, and encouraging the expression of genuine differences.

"Mediation generally involves participant empowerment, principled negotiations, and collaborative decision making. Typically, there is a facilitator, a 'neutral,' who does not have a stake in the outcome or an interest in the issue at hand. Professional mediators generally endorse one of three models: Facilitative, Evaluative or Transformative.

"In Facilitative Mediation, the mediator takes a fairly active role by asking questions, looking for underlying interests, and analyzing options. The mediator rarely proposes solutions. The common understanding is that the parties own the outcome while the mediator controls the process.

"Evaluative Mediation is different and is the form most often used by judges to reach settlement. The mediator relies upon 'shuttle diplomacy,' in which parties are separated, and the mediator goes back and forth between them. The mediator is in control of the process and has substantive influence on the outcome, by actively making proposals, evaluating fairness, and predicting the likelihood of success.

"Transformative Mediation allows participants to control both the process and the outcome, with the mediator following their lead. The goal in transformative mediation is often more about the ongoing relationships of the parties and less focused on the formal outcome. The process encourages each participant to recognize and understand the interests and needs of the other participants. They meet jointly and only separate briefly if needed.

"Purists tend to conceive of mediation as strictly falling within one of these models. In practice, the process tends to be fluid and can (or should) move freely between the approaches as appropriate."

"The process of mediation begins with introductions and an explanation of the rules of engagement. A formal introduction usually is not necessary, since we can assume everyone knows each other. But an explanation of how the process will work is crucial to ensure that everyone is operating from the same playbook.

"Even more important, participants must agree to ground rules. Usually, this starts with agreeing to basic courtesy, listening without interruption, and treating everyone with respect. In some indigenous cultures, tribal members often use a talking stick to ensure the integrity of the process for any meeting. Whoever holds the stick has the floor. No one else may talk, or interrupt, unless they have the stick, which is passed from one participant to another.

"Although I am not advocating a talking stick *per se,* there may be times when some device is necessary to ensure that each person can speak without interruption. All participants also may suggest additional rules that can be included with everyone's agreement. This is an opportunity to explain or reiterate the goal of remaining focused on the future, rather than rehashing the past."

"If emotions get in the way, *caucusing* can be an antidote. In a caucus, the mediator separates the parties and holds individual meetings with them. It's particularly useful when the high emotions are obscuring the real reasons for the mediation.

"When the process begins, every person has an uninterrupted opportunity to describe and identify issues as he or she sees them. The mediator may ask for clarification and begin to reframe the discussion to make it more neutral in tone. For example, if one member of the family says, 'He is so incompetent he can't handle running our business,' the mediator may help the speaker reframe the statement to, 'I feel I have the skills and temperament to more successfully run our business.' Such a restatement could help tone down the rhetoric and the emotional temperature of the room.

"Once every issue, however large or small, is identified, it's written down and included in an agenda to which everyone agrees. The agenda should be prominently displayed during discussions. Before tackling the first issue, the mediator will typically identify areas of agreement or common goals that became apparent during opening statements or during agenda development. This helps participants understand that they may not be as far apart as they think they are."

"It's usually productive to start with the easiest issue. If it gets resolved, there is positive momentum. Every participant—and the mediator—should brainstorm possible solutions, even if they are unworkable. The mediator lists every idea and encourages everyone to come up with more. This process continues until every possibility is exhausted, and then participants discuss what is tolerable.

"Say, for example, the parties are trying to decide what to do with the marital residence. Possible ideas could include:

- Sell it.
- Either person gets it.
- Both live in it.

- Give it to someone else, such as a child.
- Rent it.
- Tear it down and build two structures.
- Leave it empty for the time being.
- Get the equity out and buy an additional residence.

"If the parties agree to something, either fully or in part or even agree to a future process, that agreement should be written down, with everyone present endorsing both the terms and the language."

"Sometimes, however, there's no agreement that seems possible. When things come to an impasse, several techniques might help:

- The mediator might caucus separately with each participant.
- The issue might be reserved for later discussion.
- The issue might be broken into smaller issues or building blocks.
- The mediator might reframe the issue, either in general to specific or specific to general terms.
- The participants might discuss the worst alternative to not agreeing, including cost, impact on daily life, dispute escalation, and effects on other people. They might also talk about the best alternative to not agreeing, which might include continuing as is or seeking other avenues to resolve the dispute.

"This process is formal, and at times such formality might be necessary. However, the principles can be applied informally as well.

"Mediation is useful not only in resolving family disputes but also in addressing issues that don't rise to the level of conflict—at least not yet. Take, for example, the development of a prenuptial agreement. These agreements are a useful tool to address the distribution of assets and debt in the event of divorce.

"For many happily engaged couples, this limited view of a prenuptial agreement is often perceived as negative and demoralizing. It doesn't have to be. The process can enhance communication, build trust, and empower individuals. Instead of limiting prenuptial agreements to future allocation of assets and debt, prenuptial agreements can be used as a vehicle to discuss issues such as how to raise children, potential moves to other locations, taking care of aging parents, vacation planning, and so on. The list is potentially endless. Further, these agreements can be (and arguably should be) continually revisited and updated. They provide an opportunity, outside of the forum of marriage counseling or consideration of divorce, for couples to engage in a continuing process to consider their individual and mutual goals, needs, and wishes. A written contract and a semiformal process provide an opportunity for couples to reinforce their shared vision for the future—an opportunity that might otherwise be lost in the minutiae of daily life."

THE MILLER COUSINS

Three adult cousins of the third generation of a business-owning family are trying to arrange a family meeting. There has been mounting tension because of their varying needs.

One cousin wants to meet at the beach while another prefers an urban setting. One cousin has budgetary constraints while another is willing to spend well on an extravagant vacation. Each of the cousins has school-age children who are engaged in sports, camps, and other activities that restrict their availability.

Months have slid by without making a decision, and the cousins realize that another year will pass without the family meeting if they don't resolve it now. They agree to a conference call and ask a trusted family friend to participate and help them.

During the call, the friend ensures that each cousin has a full opportunity to voice their concerns and desires. They agree on the issues: timing, location, cost. They agree that timing is the easiest issue to start the discussion. After brainstorming every possibility, they discuss all the options and decide the first two weeks in August, while not perfect, is the best option.

They move on to cost, and discussion becomes heated. The family friend decides to take a break and have an individual call with one of the cousins. In the call, that cousin expresses deep frustration that one of the other cousins has not carried her weight over the years. After venting, that cousin decides that he is able to let it go and move forward because the family meeting is too important for the education of the next generation to allow it to be derailed by old resentments. The conference call resumes and the meeting is finally set.

In the sidebars are two case studies Cole supplied that demonstrate how to use mediation principles to help move a family forward.

Engaged or Inactive Family Members

Some members feel a strong pull toward the family business; they are heavily involved in the history and tradition surrounding it, and they want to remain connected to it for generations or until it is sold.

However, not all family owners wish to be actively embroiled in the family enterprise, especially as it grows and operations become more intricate and sophisticated. They may have very different interests. Cynthia, for example, is a college professor who doesn't care to be involved in the day-to-day operations of her grandfather and father's furniture empire. As a third-generation member of

THE SMITH CHILDREN

The patriarch and matriarch of the family had developed a successful family business. The father suddenly died and the mother, who was devastated by her husband's death, did not want to continue to run or be involved with the business. However, she also did not want to choose among her three adult children, so she left the decision about the business transition to the three of them. They were unable to resolve the issue and hired a mediator.

The oldest son appeared to be the responsible, controlling, and somewhat arrogant sibling who was in the best position to take over the business. The youngest child, a son, was considered to be somewhat of a ne'er-do-well, who was more interested in immediate cash and not concerned about the future sustainability of the family business. The middle child, a daughter, was the peacemaker; she preferred to avoid conflict and simply wanted everyone to get along.

The oldest brother came into the mediation with a solid plan he believed to be fair to everyone. The youngest brother continually stalled and refused to go along with the process or any alternatives. He derailed the meeting and brought the mediation session to a temporary halt.

Empowerment is an important ingredient in collaborative decision making, but power dynamics are sometimes surprising, especially in family structures. In this case, the process revealed where the power rested. The older brother was perceived by all to have the greater power in the family, but in mediation it was the younger brother who exercised the greater share of power merely by his ability to stall and thwart the process. The mediator needed to adapt to the power shift that had occurred and level the playing field accordingly.

the family, she doesn't choose to serve on the family council, but she wants to be informed about decisions that are made by the council and the company's board of directors. Although she is interested in the direction the company will take, she is an inactive owner of the family enterprise.

On the other hand, Cynthia's son Adam has an MBA, has worked in marketing in the family business for several years, and has made valuable suggestions about new product lines and channels of distribution. He can't imagine *not* being on the family council, where he feels it is his duty to serve as liaison between the board of directors and the family and to have significant input into decisions that affect both the business and those who benefit from it.

Adam is well-positioned to take over the company after his grandfather retires, and he has proven himself to be so talented that his grandfather is thinking about skipping a generation and leaving the business in his grandson's capable hands within a few years. Even if the enterprise were to be sold, Adam would maintain his place on the family council and be a leading and valuable member of the wealth management group. He is truly an active family/business member.

Neither of these positions is intrinsically wrong or right. *Inactive* is not a pejorative term. It means simply that the family member's focus is elsewhere—perhaps in a profession, another type of business, or an all-consuming avocation. It's important for the future of the family for each member to be explicit about what roles and responsibilities he or she feels comfortable assuming as the business grows or the business of family becomes more complex. It should be made clear that each member's level of participation is a choice. No family owners should be made to feel less valuable because they choose to step back from responsibilities for which they may feel unprepared or ill-equipped. Not everyone is able to succeed in business, and family members may find their vocation—what writer and theologian Frederick Buechner referred to as the meeting between a person's "deep gladness and the world's deep need"—somewhere other than in the family business.

At the far end of the spectrum of inactive family members are those who make the decision to leave the enterprise altogether. They should be allowed to do so without recrimination according to whatever terms the family has established for valuation of their share of the wealth.

Those who wish to remain engaged and have applicable skills are prime candidates for such duties as managing a portion of the business or advising those who do. They may be involved in goal-setting, hiring, decision making, document review, board or committee service, or a variety of other tasks that affect operations over months or years. They may take a leading role in negotiations if the family decides to sell the company and may continue on the corporate board once the sale is completed. Their institutional memory can be invaluable during and after the transition. They often are also leading members of the family council.

Even those who are inactive in operations have critical responsibilities to the business. These members should make it a priority to attend family meetings and become conversant with planned directions so they are not taken by surprise by decisions made by active members and/or the board. They should read and carefully examine documents the family council provides. They should ask—and receive—answers about any potential actions the board or council is anticipating. These simple steps often forestall conflict at the family meeting or in other venues. Certainly uninvolved owners may have a vote on who represents them on the family council.

Because inactive members are removed from the internal machinations of the business, they often have unique insights to bring to those who may not be able to see the forest for the trees because they are enmeshed in the details of running the company. These outside owners have a duty to share their perceptions and to talk them through with members who have decision-making powers. Their contributions may keep the business from making costly or embarrassing blunders.

Even if they choose not to take a primary role in the family business or wealth management aspects of a new fortune, it's wise for those who are uninvolved to acquaint themselves with topics that affect them as owners. They don't have to become experts, but family council decisions will make more sense if those who are not part of the business have learned the basics of subjects such as estate planning, communications, risk management, financial literacy, and investment philanthropy. The family council should make these enrichment opportunities available to develop future leaders and increase family understanding and unity. Learning together can create strong bonds and might transform inactive members into much more participatory family constituents. If the business is sold, the types of education they received prior to the sale will help make the transition from family business owners to a financial family less confusing.

It sometimes happens that as younger generations of the family mature, they may want to move from a place of inactivity to become engaged owners. Those who have been active for many years may wish to scale back their involvement. Governance documents should spell out the manner in which these types of transfers can occur.

In short, all family members have important roles to fill. Even if they do not participate in the business itself, their value may lie in their questions, life experience, loyalty to the legacy, networks, soft skills and talents, or myriad other strengths. All should be encouraged to bring their gifts to the table and to share them for the benefit of the whole.

In the beginning, some members may resist the introduction of formal governance into family matters, but in time, when hard questions are asked, answered, and resolved, when relationships blossom, and when values pass seamlessly from one generation to the next, most families are glad they took the time to codify their beliefs and practices.

Notes

1. "2014 Family Business Survey—Up Close and Professional: The Family Factor," www.pwc.com/gx/en/services/family-business/family-business-survey.html. Retrieved May 16, 2016.
2. Lisa Gray, *Generational Wealth Management* (London: Euromoney Trading, Ltd., 2010), p. 149.

3. Ibid., p. 149.
4. Ibid., p. 163.
5. Ibid., p. 164.
6. John Ward, www.thefbcg.com/The-Roles-and-Responsibilities-of-Family-Own ership, The Family Business Consulting Group. Retrieved May 17, 2016.
7. Ibid.
8. James E. Hughes Jr., *Family Wealth: Keeping It in the Family* (New York: Bloomberg Press, 2004), p. 21.
9. Ibid.

CHAPTER 9

Developing Future Leadership

The entrepreneurial ventures that grow into multimillion-dollar businesses usually are founded by one person, or perhaps a couple of family members from one or two generations. The founders are the natural leaders of an enterprise built on their dreams, ideas, and sweat. However, the qualities that make for great entrepreneurs often are not the attributes that sustain a fortune, a family, or even a business through multiple generations.

Open almost any list that details the traits shared by entrepreneurs and you'll find characteristics such as passion, tolerance for risk and uncertainty, creativity and open-mindedness, goal direction, hands-on management style, and commitment to the business.

In general, these traits are highly positive. However, over time, as they become "the way we do things," a flipside may emerge, as illustrated by the following table.

Trait	Result	Flipside	Result
Passion	Energy and excitement about the venture.	Superficial understanding of market conditions, timing, and economics. Unreal expectations about one's chances for huge, quick success. Belief that the only thing needed is a great idea and plenty of drive. May choose partners/associates based on their eagerness to build the business rather than their ability to do so.	Lack of life balance. Unhappy family members as they take second position to the business venture.

Trait	Result	Flipside	Result
Tolerance for risk/ uncertainty	Ability to see beyond current contingencies to final success.	Quick, perhaps rash, decisions.	Business failure because of not correctly reading signs of impending problems.
Creativity/ open-mindedness	Can incorporate new ideas quickly to improve product or service.	Too many ideas at once; inability to see a way forward from possible options.	Stagnation because an idea may not be tried out sufficiently before moving on to the next strategy.
Goal direction	Focus on and progress toward ultimate success.	Overly narrow concentration that crowds out good ideas and suggestions from others.	Slower than anticipated growth. Insistence on "the one best way" to reach the goal.
Hands-on management style	Infuses others with entrepreneurial passion.	Dictatorial leadership.	High levels of conflict. Exodus of talented associates who feel discounted and disrespected. Lack of leadership preparation of new family members because they are not permitted to test their skills.
Commitment to the business	Lights a fire under associates.	Rigidity.	Expects unrealistic levels of performance from others. Loses those who think of their work as a job or profession rather than as their self-definition.

In short, most entrepreneurs are doers, and as the business grows, they need to balance their hands-on orientation with those who are thinkers and others who perhaps have a wider worldview and different, complementary skills.

These same conditions apply to the management of wealth. In the beginning, the wealth creator usually rules. However, managing wealth in a growing, diverse, and disparate family is too complex for one or two people. Almost inevitably there comes a day when the wealth creator becomes less interested in the daily operations of the business, wants to move on to exciting new ventures, or begins to see retirement as a desirable option. If next-generation leadership has not been selected and groomed for new responsibilities, the business is ripe for failure even before the third generation.

Long-term family sustainability of wealth in all its forms requires consistent and effective leadership by current family members and their outside advisors, if any, and careful, purposeful development of leadership in the following generations. Successful leaders generally are not born; they may have leadership potential, but that potential can languish if not recognized and cultivated.

Families who have successfully sustained wealth understand that thoughtful and well-organized leadership development adds value, and they seek to identify and prepare potential future leaders.

Similar to business organizations that strive to sustain themselves over time, families benefit by implementing time-tested processes and tools that (1) can assess leadership potential, (2) determine gaps or weaknesses, and (3) create development programs to promote excellence in areas such as business skills, communications, emotional intelligence, organization, and the art and science of leading others.

Many families have been introduced to The Clifton Strengthsfinder™, an assessment tool published by Gallup Press and used to identify thirty-four different "talent themes" or strengths. The Strengthsfinder website explains that "talents are people's naturally recurring patterns of thought, feeling, or behavior that can be productively applied. The more dominant a theme is in a person, the greater the theme's impact on that person's behavior and performance."[1] They include strengths in areas such as communication, organization, strategy, and a wide range of other critical abilities.

Strengths Based Leadership by Tom Rath and Barry Conchie posits four types of leadership strength: executing, influencing, relationship building, and strategic thinking. The thirty-four Strengthsfinder themes are arranged under these domains.[2] For example, an empathetic person could be strong in relationship-building, an analytical family member might be useful in creating strategy, and an adept communicator could be helpful in influencing others. Learning each member's top five strengths can be eye-opening for families and help each one appreciate the others' talents as the family goes about generating its financial and personal legacies. Such understanding creates coherence and a climate conducive to sustaining wealth.

A variety of other tools are available not only to spot talent and leadership potential, but also to point out preferred ways of being. The venerable Myers-Briggs Type Indicator can be helpful in sorting out why certain members of the family have difficulty working together, even if they are generally in agreement and of good will toward one another. An introvert, for example, may tire at a family meeting just at the time the extravert is warming up. Knowing that these differences are matters of psychological style rather than areas of disagreement can go a long way to defusing situations that might otherwise spin out of control.

It's usually best for a trained facilitator to administer inventories like these, because they are proficient in interpreting the results and assisting the group in understanding how the knowledge gained can be applied most effectively. They can help highlight talents the family might have overlooked and how those talents can be useful in furthering the family enterprise.

Where Are the Leaders?

Today's family leaders come from every generation. New creators of wealth still may be heading their companies. Second-generation members often have taken the reins while third-generation potential leaders may be champing at the bit for their chance to excel. Of course, in long-lived companies, fourth-, fifth-, and sixth-generation members of the family assumed positions of leadership years ago. All these people may exhibit greater or lesser degrees of family leadership prowess, but a strong, effective leader does the following:

- Focuses on family accomplishments, rather than personal aggrandizement. A true leader feels successful when his or her team, in this case the family, succeeds.
- Is guided by the vision and mission the family has hammered out together.
- Models integrity; that is, can be counted on to adhere to the same moral and ethical code no matter what the situation.
- Looks beyond the numbers. Of course, continuing financial growth is the engine that makes it possible for the family to be engaged in activities that have meaning for them, but if wealth is more than money (and it is), the good leader also is driven by the family interests, which may include philanthropy, impact investment, legacy, or any combination.

- Demonstrates respect for all members of the family and understands that their various gifts are useful at different times and stages and for different purposes.
- Is a trustworthy mentor for those who are interested in taking an active role in the family but who need appropriate guidance.
- Is clear and self-possessed in communicating with the family, whether the news is good or bad.
- Is a creative thinker who can generate alternative solutions to thorny dilemmas.
- Can call on sharply honed people skills and street smarts to accomplish objectives.
- Exhibits high emotional intelligence; that is, can recognize, understand, and manage his or her own emotions and recognize, understand, and influence the emotions of others.
- Is aware that consensus is hard to achieve without careful listening for commonalities among disparate opinions and is willing to take the time to search for such areas of agreement. The strong leader brings his or her emotional intelligence to this task, often with highly positive results.
- Doesn't duck controversies, but anticipates and deals with them calmly and in consultation with those who are affected by them.
- Is comfortable interacting with all types of family members—engaged, disinterested, owners, nonowners—from every generation.
- Exhibits a growth, rather than a fixed, mindset, which allows the leader to learn from errors rather than be stymied by setbacks. Watching a leader grapple with tough challenges from a growth perspective can be a powerful motivator for those who want to learn how to lead.

Daniell and Hamilton also mention the need for the leader to have a sense of humor, a feeling of gratitude for the family's good fortune, and empathy for others. They add, "By reaching the hearts as well as the minds and financial interest of family members ... an effective leader may be able to release new levels of energy to contribute to a family's current and future prosperity."[3]

Obviously, it's rare for any one leader to embody all the leadership traits mentioned in the extensive list above, but the list shows us the importance of what are sometimes called "soft skills." Although it is essential for family wealth management leaders to be conversant with the tactical aspects of the task—tax and estate planning, investment policies, accounting, asset allocation, and more—those skills make for a great technician, but not necessarily a great leader. The combination of a tactical perspective and at least a few of the qualitative characteristics noted above are the marks of an admirable leader and role model for those coming along behind. Of course, if there's a void in a particular leadership domain, a talent identification program such as Strengthsfinder 2.0 can assist the family in finding those who have those particular skills.

Building Leadership

Leaders cannot be developed if they are hamstrung by a "do-it-my-way-or-else" founder. Although it may be hard for the wealth creator to cede any control, Stephen P. Miller suggests that family climate has a sizable impact on whether new leadership will be permitted to take root and thrive. "A family climate characterized by open communication, shared values and norms, and a senior generation that devotes attention to the welfare, needs and concerns of the younger generation is more likely to produce next-generation leaders who accept responsibility for their ... actions and decisions."[4] Conversely, he mentions that a family climate based on authoritarian rule will produce rising leaders who "shun responsibility" and are less competent largely because they may be afraid to lead.

Learning to Lead

An emerging leader needs four things: innate characteristics that show the spark of leadership, opportunities to lead, a willingness to learn, and mentors to show the way.

Research reported in an online article published by *Harvard Business Review* stated that when looking for new leadership, "values seem to be the acid test. ... We found a 95% overlap in the language that each firm's family members and nonfamily executives used to describe their corporate ethos: words such as *respect, integrity, quality, humility, passion, modesty,* and *ambition.*"[5]

Other desirable qualities for upcoming leaders include the following:

- A reverence for the family history and previous leaders, but the resolve not to be hamstrung by the founder's dream. In short, a combination of appreciation for tradition and a future orientation.
- A strong belief in their own abilities, tempered with the knowledge that they will make errors that may be costly. They exhibit a determination to learn from their mistakes rather than be undone by them.
- A willingness to collaborate and share credit. Conversely, leaders show an equal willingness to take the hit if one of their decisions turns out badly.
- Sufficient experience in either the family business or an outside company.

As Denise Kenyon-Rouvinez and Anne-Catrin Glemser pointed out, "Next-generation members who enter the family firm right after . . . university receive training from the bottom up and build credibility within both the business and the family. . . . On the other hand, gaining external experience with an unrelated corporation supports [their . . . development] by building credibility, self-confidence and networks."[6]

Some families encourage both by offering family business internships and negotiating with another family to set up internships within each other's businesses. In this way, younger generations see there's more than one way to run a successful enterprise. Other families might look for international internships in similar businesses. Such internships not only allow students to see how business is done in another country but also develop invaluable appreciation for the roles of language and culture in conducting business in our wired and interconnected world.

As the current generations evaluate the next crop of potential leaders, they might look for these important criteria for leadership. The most important question to be answered is whether the candidates *want* to take a leadership role in the family. Willingness is crucial. Not every talented next-gen member has a desire to excel in the family business or wishes to have a big say in how the family wealth is managed. Some of the reasons for their reluctance might stem from the following:

- A desire to lead a different lifestyle from the rest of the family. Someone who has chosen to be a doctor may have little desire to be part of the leadership team at an energy company.
- A fear that they will have to work much harder than others simply because they are family members and have to prove themselves worthy of their positions.
- A worry that other family members will be jealous because of the new leader's "preferred status."
- Trepidation about being swallowed up by the business and the expectation that anyone carrying the family name must have an overwhelming interest in the company the family founded and built.

If, however, members of the rising generation want to lead, the current leaders should examine the follow issues:

- Do the candidates demonstrate by word and example a real dedication to the family?
- Are they motivated to work hard to develop their leadership capabilities?
- Do they exhibit the ability to influence others?

- Are they both aspirational and inspirational?
- Do they have new ideas or new twists on how to make time-tested ideas better?
- Do they already have well-developed communication skills?
- Do they manage conflict well?
- Are they willing and eager to accept mentoring by other members of the family or other trusted advisors?
- Do they have the character and empathy to understand others?
- Do they have the requisite tactical skills? In what areas of the business or wealth management do they excel?

It is not enough to identify these potential leaders, however. The family now has an obligation to educate and train them for upcoming areas of responsibility. That training may come in a variety of ways. The younger members might be sponsored for institutes or postgraduate programs at institutions such as the Kellogg School of Management, the Wharton School of the University of Pennsylvania, the University of Chicago Booth School of Business, the Family Office Exchange, the Stetson Family Enterprise Center, the Institute for Private Investors, and the Transitions East and Transitions West Conferences.

Leadership training programs could become a regular feature of family meetings. Webinars and other online options can be helpful for understanding in specific leadership disciplines. Internal or external coaching can be very effective. Internal coaches have wide knowledge of the family business while external coaches bring "greater objectivity, fresher perspective, higher levels of confidentiality, and experience in many different organizations, industries, and business environments."[7]

In addition, talented younger members may serve on various family committees, such as the family council, the family foundation if one exists, family research committee, finance and investment committee, or as a liaison to the family office. These exposures will bring them a wide knowledge of family concerns, obligations, history, and ongoing issues.

Some families place younger members on a junior board, which is elected by and represents the interests of the younger generations. As Barbara Hauser explained, the junior board "follow[s] the procedural rules of the main board and act[s] as ... liaison [to them].... A junior board member attends each of the main board meetings as a non-voting participant. The junior board then has a chance to discuss the issues, and its comments are reported ... to the main board."[8]

The back-and-forth between the main and junior boards allows younger members to learn, but also to contribute new ideas. The interchange can be enlivening and bring exciting new possibilities to the surface for consideration by the main board or the entire family.

Of course, all the training in the world means nothing if the next-gen leaders aren't given responsibilities that are appropriate for their stage of development and that stretch them slightly past their current capabilities. Letting go of the management of a piece of the family business or wealth (or both) requires a leap of faith on the part of those already in charge and a willingness to mentor, perhaps from a distance, as the new leader learns the ropes. Failure must be an option. If people never are allowed to fail, they never learn to be resilient and try new ways to solve problems.

However the family governance apparatus is structured, being part of these committees and councils helps a new generation of potential leaders become aware of the many roles and avenues of service that may await them. When they find the right fit, they also may find a life of great satisfaction.

The Best Mentors

Those who mentor the next generation may be family members or outside-the-family advisors. Whoever they are, they should be:

- Willing to take the time required to prepare a new family leader. Mentorship is not a one-and-done. It's a relationship that requires a desire to watch a younger or less-experienced person develop, grow, and eventually thrive.
- Able to communicate clearly.
- Discreet and trustworthy. In the mentor relationship, the one who is mentored may share his or her fears and insecurities, and these confidences must not be shared.
- Honest. Those who are being mentored deserve and should expect honest appraisals of their qualities, skills, talents, and areas for improvement. The purpose of mentorship is growth, not flattery.
- Knowledgeable. Good mentors know what their mentees need to know, and if they don't, they are confident enough to bring in other resources to help.
- Compassionate and empathetic. People make mistakes and learn at different rates, and life sometimes throws them off track. Though not a patsy, a good mentor makes allowances if someone doesn't live up to expectations every time.
- A learner. Great mentors understand that lessons come in all shapes and sizes and that knowledge flows in both directions. They are humble enough to learn something from those they mentor.

It is rare for a family to be headed by only one leader. Even the single entrepreneur who amasses the family fortune may be aided by an unsung person, sometimes a spouse or old and trusted friend, who backstops the leader. As the family grows, a leadership team becomes more and more critical. A process to continually bring new leadership to the fore is essential.

Notes

1. www.strengthstest.com/strengths-finder-themes.
2. Tom Rath and Barry Conchie, *Strength Based Leadership: Great Leaders, Teams and Why People Follow Them* (New York: Gallup Press, 2008).
3. Mark Haynes Daniell and Sarah S. Hamilton, *Family Legacy and Leadership: Preserving True Family Wealth in Challenging Times* (Asia: John Wiley & Sons, 2010).
4. Stephen P. Miller, "Developing Next-Generation Leaders in Family Business," www.thefbcg.com/developing-next-generation-leaders-in-family-business. Retrieved June 1, 2016.
5. Claudio Fernández-Aráoz, Sonny Iqbal, and Jörg Ritter, "Leadership Lessons from Great Family Businesses," *Harvard Business Review* (April 2015), hbr.org/2015/04/leadership-lessons-from-great-family-businesses. Retrieved June 3, 2016.
6. Denise Kenyon-Rouvinez and Anne-Catrin Glemser, "To Be, or Not to Be, The Next-Generation Family Business Leader: Four Questions Younger Family Members Should Ask Themselves," www.imd.org/research/challenges/TC052-14-next-generation-family-business-leader-kenyon-rouvinez-glemser.cfm. Retrieved June 5, 2016.
7. "Coaching: A Global Study of Successful Practices: Current Trends and Future Possibilities 2008–2018," www.opm.gov/WIKI/uploads/docs/Wiki/OPM/training/i4cp-coaching.pdf. Retrieved June 7, 2016.
8. Barbara R. Hauser, "The Child Garden" (November 2013), www.brhauser.com/articles/the%20child%20garden%20step%20eight%20ways.pdf. Retrieved September 22, 2016.

CHAPTER 10

Family Education: Building a Culture of Learning and Continuous Improvement

The previous chapter highlighted the importance of family leadership. The fact is, however, that not every member of a family is equipped to be—or wishes to be—a leader. Nonetheless, *all* of the current and future owners, stakeholders, and beneficiaries of the wealth need to build and sustain a foundation of strategic and tactical wealth management knowledge to ensure multigenerational sustainability and success. If family members possess only scant awareness of such issues as diversification, asset allocation, and long-term investment plans, and they have only limited skills in communication, the results can be disastrous. They may find themselves the victims of risky, concentrated positions in sectors they don't understand. They may make the decision to value quick gains and instant gratification, which results in the rapid dissipation of the family's wealth. They might insist on greater current liquidity rather than the steady growth provided by a sound investment strategy. They may not understand the importance of their participation in family decisions. All of these deficiencies will damage the viability of the family enterprise.

Education is crucial. Successful families—those that have broken the "shirtsleeves to shirtsleeves" wealth problem—have developed mores that include ongoing education and continuous improvement as a family. This process is not a crash diet or a one-time event, but a continual process for the entire family, beginning with the youngest members and involving every generation of the family.

In *People* magazine's excerpt from *The Rainbow Comes and Goes: A Mother and Son on Life, Love, and Loss,* Anderson Cooper asked his ninety-one-year-old mother, Gloria Vanderbilt, if she had been prepared to inherit $4.5 million when she turned twenty-one. "Hard to believe," she responded, "but no one had ever discussed this inheritance with me. I wish I had known then that the greatest gift of money is the independence it can give you. . . . The money I've earned through work is the only money I respect."[1]

The situation in which Vanderbilt found herself is not unusual. Even today, families often wait too long to prepare future heirs for their ultimate bequests and all the responsibilities and opportunities that come with them.

However, delaying the development and implementation of a thoughtful and well-designed program of preparation can lead to the exact results families are looking to avoid. In fact, the outcomes from a lack of careful preparation can include confusion, anger, conflict, poor decision making, lost opportunities, and even negative behaviors such as addiction.

Preparing the Kids

Suppose you're a bright but self-conscious thirteen-year-old boy attending a private school in the upper Midwest. You know your parents are, as they have told you, "comfortable," or "well-off," or even "blessed." But that's all you know. One of your classmates, however, has taken it upon himself to conduct background research on every member of the class. From easily accessible Web resources, he has discovered what your parents paid for your house and even its square footage. He knows what they shell out in property taxes each year. In the financial news, he's read that your mother's father started the business your father has built into a multinational firm employing hundreds of people. He has extrapolated the value of the stock your family holds in the company. He's found an online article that places your family fortune at well over $70 million and decides to share the relative financial standing of every member of the class in a newsletter he places on each desk. Your name is at the top of the list. You are mortified as only a young teen can be. Confused and enraged, you ask your parents why they never told you any of this.

A T. Rowe Price *Parents, Kids, and Money Survey* conducted in 2015 reported that 18 percent of parents are very or extremely reluctant to discuss financial matters with their kids, and 72 percent are at least somewhat reluctant to speak about them. The reasons for this reluctance ranged from a high of "I don't want them to worry about money" (52 percent) to a low of

"It's none of their business" (13 percent). Nearly 25 percent worried that their children would share sensitive family information with others.

Most wealthy parents don't voice these exact sentiments, but many don't talk about their finances with their children because they don't want to sap their kids' initiative and drive by allowing them to know they might not ever have to work for a living.

The reluctance mentioned in the study also may be a hangover from the days when religion, politics, and money were topics not to be discussed in polite society. That time has passed. With the advent of instantaneous online information-sharing, almost anyone can find out anything. And those referred to as digital natives, a term that includes tech-savvy children, are among the most proficient information-gatherers around. They may not always make the wisest use of what they unearth, but they know how to dig it out. Rich children may be far more aware of their situation than their parents suspect, and they may be uneasy about what they know.

Outworn attitudes must shift with the times. Children who are members of wealthy families must be prepared for their financial futures, but it's about more than money. It's also about preparing them for lives of meaning and purpose—and the independence Gloria Vanderbilt mentioned. Depending on how information is handled, great wealth allows children to soar or leaves them confused and at risk.

Children, even siblings, may have very different understandings of money. Trey,* a college student, watched his father struggle for fifteen years to maintain and build a family business established by the young man's grandfather. Many of Trey's attitudes about money probably were formed by watching his father work days, nights, and weekends. Perhaps he has come to value that kind of dedication and the resilience his father showed when things weren't going his way. On the other hand, he may believe that his father sorely neglected the family, and his feelings about the acquisition and use of wealth may be tinged with resentment about his dad's absence from many special family occasions.

Three years ago, when Trey entered college, his father sold the business for more than $70 million. Trey's youngest sibling, Melissa,* was eight years old when this liquidity event occurred, and since then she has had the opportunity to spend lots of time with her father. She is generally unaware of the disappointments and setbacks Trey witnessed as he grew up. Her father is able to attend her soccer games and school events. Melissa has everything she wants, including a relationship with her dad that Trey sometimes envies.

---

*The examples with an asterisk mentioned in this chapter are composites of cases the author has encountered in his wealth management career. Names and all identifying details have been changed to protect privacy.

Trey's family's wealth came quickly, a situation that offers a different set of challenges from those experienced by families who have managed wealth as a group over several generations. No matter how the wealth was gained, however, sustaining it requires care, patience, and education.

Money and Values

"While parents may have good intentions for raising money-mature kids, they often fail to succeed because they don't move from soft intentions to a realized program of financial education tailored to the age and interests of the children," said Lewis Schiff.[2] That program must begin while the child is young, continue into adulthood, and, as Schiff says, be wrapped around the student's particular interests. Children are different in temperaments and passions, and nothing engages them more quickly than seeing how the family wealth can help them achieve what matters to them, whether that's philanthropy, artistic pursuits, an MBA or other professional degree, worldwide ecotourism, a career in public service, or, for youngsters, even paying for their own bicycle.

Of course, any type of education must be age-appropriate. Some experts suggest that the first money talk take place before the age of ten. Naturally, children that age won't understand the ins and outs of wealth management, but most of them, even of relatively tender years, understand that they have more than many other people. Lectures about money itself usually aren't very effective, but casual conversations around the dining room table or on a family outing can introduce important family lore about how the privileges the children enjoy came to be.

Children love stories, and most wealth histories have some exciting elements: the family's arrival in the United States, the renegade uncle whose creative idea saved the company during an economic downturn, the great-aunt who reared six children alone and kept the business going after the death of her husband, or the cousin who donated all his land as a nature preserve. When parents talk about money in the context of family's values such as perseverance, loyalty, unity, and generosity, it helps children learn that money is a tool to make things happen, not an end in itself.

Such an introduction to the positive aspects of wealth serves as the foundation for slow, steady continuing education based on the child's social and emotional readiness.

Financial games can be the springboard to conversations about wealth. Board games such as the classic Monopoly can teach children the risks and rewards of both aggressive and conservative approaches to acquiring and managing wealth. They can also learn about borrowing, lending, and mortgages, all in a fun, engaging way. Of course, a worldwide digital version of the game is available, but to encourage conversation and family understanding, nothing beats a face-to-face contest, unimpeded by a screen. Often, children who scoff at "analog" games end up enjoying the interchange with parents and become eager to play.

In a Bloomberg Advantage radio podcast, Kathy Lintz, managing director of Matter Family Office, talked about educating children as young as four to five years of age and providing "skills, values, communication programs, and knowledge that create the infrastructure … that helps wealth become sustainable."[3]

Lintz's family education about allowances, for example, helps children understand the concept of allowance and additional earnings. "Allowance is not to be confused with family obligation…. It's not tied to behaviors, (sic) it's a way to share in the family resources, values, and money management practices."[4] Earning money, on the other hand, *is* linked with behavior: chores for younger children and jobs for those who are older. The download for this teaching and learning program includes a sample allowance contract and interesting ways parents, if they choose, can enhance children's earnings and teach them about banking and credit.

Many other programs are available to give children a wider understanding of their financial lives. Themint.org offers an array of activities in Fun for Kids, Tips for Teens, and Pointers for Parents. For computer-literate kids (and that's most of them), a plethora of age-appropriate apps help children and adults converse about money in a way that is comfortable for both.[5] The well-known ThreeJars program "is built on the idea that kids can learn to manage money in an easy, useful, even fun way."[6]

Among the most common requirements of a financial literacy program such as ThreeJars is that money the youngster is given as an allowance, earns through household or neighborhood chores, or receives as gifts be divided into three categories: spend, save, and share (or donate). Others may add a fourth category: invest. By choosing what amounts go into which categories, the child learns the value of thrift, the impact of saving, the rewards of delayed gratification, and the pleasure of helping others. If the children choose the invest category, the parent may add a small percentage to demonstrate how investments grow.

However, all the talk in the world means nothing if parents don't model the values they purport to espouse. A child who overhears an adult tell a lie learns that honesty is important—except when it isn't. A child who witnesses a parent breaking a confidence as she gossips about a friend will learn that secrets are not inviolate. A child who sees a parent mistreat a housekeeper or the waitstaff in a restaurant learns that manners are dispensable.

Parents' attitudes toward wealth influence their children, too. Why should a child not request $300 shoes or the most extravagant kindergarten birthday party in the city if Mom replaces her entire wardrobe every three months or Dad buys a new Ferrari in even-numbered years? Conversely, if parents are involved—and involve the children—in philanthropy or impact investment and share the reasons why the adults have made these choices, it's more likely the kids will see the use of money as a tool for good rather than simply a source of instant gratification. Children learn what they live, and parents are the most powerful role models of all.

As Helene W. Stein and Marcia C. Brier said in a 2001 article that is still applicable today, "[Parents] must take a look at how they spend their money … and ask, 'Is this what I want my children to do?' If the answer is 'No,' parents may need to make some changes in their own financial life and in their own behavior."[7]

As the children mature and show a desire to understand what the family values, parents may involve them more directly in organizations they support. For example, if the family underwrites a large local hunger initiative, children can help bag groceries at a pantry, meeting face to face with recipients who deal with food insecurity every day. Those who would rather be outside could work at a community garden that supplies fresh food for those in need. Ten-to twelve-year-olds often love to serve or clean up at a weekly dinner for those who otherwise might not have a meal. These types of hands-on experiences give them an up-close-and-personal understanding of issues they otherwise might have seen only on the news.

Some wealthy families expose their children to the problems of the wider world as well. Philanthropic parents who have established organizations to dig wells, build schools, or provide health care in underdeveloped nations sometimes take their children with them on visits to these locales, perhaps halfway around the world. The effects are at least eye-opening and sometimes overpowering, and the children may grow up to take an active role in these endeavors.

When they are old enough to understand the lesson, children also should spend time in the business that has provided their wealth. This familiarization with the family firm helps them understand that the money they enjoy is not happenstance or a lucky fluke but the result of a great deal of effort by family members and others who work for the company. They will learn to prize the contributions all these people have made to the family's financial well-being, which may make them better, more appreciative company officers if and when they take their place in the family business—or even if they are passive owners. Parents should model an attitude of humility and kindness toward employees during these encounters so the children don't develop an attitude that "all these people work for *me!*"

Managing Money: Younger Children

Some advisors suggest that all children be given a modest allowance and that it be increased over time as the child grows and demonstrates greater maturity. Sometimes parents tie the allowance to chores, but that may be a difficult concept for children to understand if they are being reared in a family with a household staff. Others may give the allowance solely to encourage financial education.

Managing Money: Older Children

When young people are learning lessons about money, they must be permitted to fail. Perhaps they've been saving for the highest-end video-gaming system or putting aside money for an over-the-top designer prom dress. If they blow those savings on first-row tickets to the hottest concert of the year, the parents must resist buying the saved-for items, even if their first instinct is to rush in and salve the kids' disappointment that they can't everything they want. Actions have consequences, but if natural consequences are not allowed to run their course, these adults-in-training learn nothing except that Mom and Dad will rescue them every time they make a decision they later regret— and that's the beginning of an entitled attitude.

If the next generation has absorbed earlier monetary lessons and is demonstrating sufficient maturity and responsibility (which usually occurs around the age of majority), many parents introduce their children to the family's financial advisors. Working with the parents, these advisors can become part of a structured program of education in investment, philanthropy, the roles of trustees and beneficiaries, and more. If they are careful listeners, interested in the children's hopes and dreams for their futures, good mentors and teachers, highly skilled in their areas of expertise, working together as a team, and dedicated to the entire family's best interests, these professionals can go a long way toward helping the family realize its goal of wealth sustainability and amity over many generations.

Adults, Too

It's not only rising generations who require education. If the wealth creators and their families are not steeped in financial expertise, the adults also need to learn about every aspect of wealth management, not once and for all, but continually. The economic and business environment changes rapidly, and high-net-worth families should have financial advisors who teach them how to be effective stewards of their wealth and how to navigate conditions that are sure to change.

The advisor/advisee relationship is a two-way street. Good advisors do not take control and ramrod their strategies through the family. Instead, they listen to their clients' wealth objectives, what values they want to personify, and what unique issues and challenges the family faces. They work as partners with the family to design and implement the strategies that will ensure the goals are met, consulting with the family often and keeping them informed every step of the way. They maintain relationships with other advisors to avoid duplication of efforts, risky asset allocation or unintended concentrations, and other unpleasant surprises.

To develop a well-structured, generationally specific, ongoing educational program, families and their advisors must consider both qualitative and quantitative elements. Here are seven of the key strategic elements:

1. *The meaning of money:* Education surrounding the meaning of money takes into account the fact that money is neutral. It becomes positive or negative based on the family's use of its resources and whether that use is in accord with the family's stated values and beliefs.

2. *Spending, saving, and giving:* The family may have adopted the Three-Jars approach for children, but as a collective entity, the family should be educated as to best practices in saving, spending, investing, and philanthropy. The educational program should include tactical dimensions such as the tax ramifications of every type of financial decision, as well as the importance of the strategic aspects.

3. *The history of the family and the wealth:* As discussed previously, an understanding of the wealth story is often the glue that holds the family together, and the family members could either hire someone to do the work and provide a family history or they could, with some assistance, research records themselves and become responsible for learning and sharing the family lore.

4. *The family enterprise:* Much of the education in this sector depends on whether the family is still a business-owning group or a financial family.

5. *Entrepreneurship and the role of private capital:* Most family fortunes are built on the entrepreneurial genius of the wealth creator. Advisors can help the family recapture or polish the legacy by educating the family as to how private capital can be used to seize entrepreneurial opportunities.

6. *Family roles and responsibilities:* Education around these issues should include discovering the strengths of all family members, whether they choose to be active or passive participants in the family enterprise.

Opportunities for continuing education can be explored and succession planning initiated or expanded.

7. *Family vision and values:* The family will need to learn best practices in creating and maintaining the common vision and mission and how to handle disagreements if decisions appear to be violating these foundational principles.

The more tactical issues include:

- Cash flow and budgeting
- Banking
- Investment management
- Tax planning
- Estate planning
- Philanthropy

Each of the tactical pieces of the puzzle is considered in greater depth in Chapter 12.

As indicated earlier in this chapter, the programming must be customized for each generation and the specific requirements and circumstances of each family. The Family Office Exchange notes that in creating a family education plan, "respect for individual readiness, learning styles, and unique needs, balanced by the imperative to be 'on a journey' will help ensure success for family learning and legacy."[8]

As long as the family education plan is carefully created to be ongoing and coherent, there's nothing in the *Great Big Book of Wealth Management* that says the educational opportunities have to be dull and boring. In fact, learning that takes place in the context of enjoyment can be much more lasting than sitting at a family meeting with a notebook full of graphs and charts. A family retreat featuring age-appropriate fun and lots of opportunity for multigenerational conversation creates understanding and an atmosphere conducive to inquiry and decision making. Education can take place during family retreats or meetings in locations as varied as the Appalachians, the Andes, or the Alps. The very wealthy have considerable choice in when, where, and how they learn what they need to know.

As part of their governance structure, many families set up an education committee comprising a few family members, or they retain a coordinator to develop the program. Their professional advisory team also may help design and implement the curriculum. During their experience of working with the family, the professionals may have gained insights into the family's knowledge gaps; they can then suggest what issues should be addressed to boost the levels of understanding and create educational offerings that reflect the learning styles and financial sophistication of every family group.

However the family chooses to structure its education plan, it's a vital part of the wealth management process and should not be ignored.

Notes

1. "Family Secrets," *People* (April 11, 2016), p. 74.
2. Lewis Schiff, "Wealth Management Insider, Unprepared Children of High Net Worth Clients: How Financial Education Can Not Only Help the Children but Also Support the Work of Advisors," www.aicpastore.com/Content/media/ PRODUCER_CONTENT/Newsletters/Articles_2011/Wealth/High-Net-Worth_Clients.jsp, March 17, 2011. Retrieved June 21, 2016.
3. Matter Family Office, www.matterfamilyoffice.com/blog/kathy-lintz-discusses-delayed-gratification-summer-jobs-allowance-bloomberg-radio/.
4. Ibid.
5. Allana Akhtar, "7 Apps to Teach Your Kids Personal Finance Skills," *U.S. News and World Report—Money* (June 23, 2015). Retrieved September 21, 2016.
6. ThreeJars website, www.threejars.com/home.
7. Helene W. Stein and Marcia C. Brier, "Raising Responsible Children of Wealth," WealthManagement.com (May 22, 2001), wealthmanagement.com/ news/raising-responsible-children-wealth-1. Retrieved June 21, 2016.
8. Teresa Bellock, "The Family Office Exchange," www.familyoffice.com/insights/ education-key-your-familys-financial-future. Retrieved June 24, 2016.

CHAPTER 11

Communication and Alignment: Working Together as a High-Functioning Team

Perhaps the biggest detriment to successful long-term wealth management is lack of timely, consistent, and appropriate communications to family members, based on their roles in the family, their levels of sophistication, and their personal preferences and requirements. As indicated in Chapter 1, we know that 60 percent of the failures in multigenerational wealth management are due to lack of communication and trust among family members. Even with these daunting statistics in mind, few families develop an effective family communication plan that provides important information and helps to maintain family harmony and coordination.

In fact, the 2007 Mass Mutual American Family Business Survey indicated that by 2017, 40.3 percent of family business owners expected to retire, but fewer than half of those planning to do so even five years earlier had selected a successor.[1] Generally, that lack of planning and communication guarantees disaster—and perhaps loss of the business followed by the subsequent loss of the family fortune.

When the assets are under the domain and management of the wealth creator, there is often little communication about the wealth, and what information is shared trickles down from the top. Over time, however, as the number of family members grows exponentially, communication can become garbled and lead to misunderstandings and discord. A well-organized communication plan is critical if the family wants to continue managing wealth as a shared resource.

Ideally, the communication plan is not an off-the-shelf solution. It is customized for each family based on the family's size, extent of geographic dispersal, and preferences. The plan can include family meetings, reports, newsletters, and closed websites, among other options. It also may extend not only to family members, but also to shared employees, professional advisors, and service providers. The plan should be reviewed and modified periodically as needs change.

The communication process and its protocols allow the family members who have ownership rights to stay informed and engaged and to feel a sense of accountability. With an effective communication platform in place, both those in a position of management and those in a position of ownership have a clear understanding of what to expect—and when. Meeting these expectations reduces the possibility of miscommunication, friction, or outright conflict.

In the previous chapter, the topic was primarily how to prepare succeeding generations to inherit. However, there's much more to family communication than parent–child conversations. Open, clear, and honest adult communication is essential for individual family units and the family as a whole. Differing viewpoints inevitably arise in any group of people trying to arrive at consensus around sensitive issues, and such topics can be even more difficult to resolve in a family setting as members strive to avoid disagreements or hurt feelings, or, alternatively, erupt into angry altercations.

Who Needs to Be Heard?

As Sylvia Shepherd mentioned in "Representing Family Constituencies: The Role of the Family Council,"[2] each family has a variety of constituencies within its make-up. Gathered together, these "multiple, overlapping" constituencies can create a tangled web of interests and emphases. Shepherd mentions family branches, those who have married into the family, women, those working in the business ("insiders"), those with no ties to those who work for the business ("outsiders"), different generations, and minority shareholders as the constituencies of her family council. Each of the constituencies may have very different communication needs. For example, Shepherd noted, those who work in the business have access to information the rest of the family doesn't. They have little need for the types of communication the other family members require to stay up to date about the actions of the council.

Communication between and among family branches becomes more complex as the family grows. In the second generation, sibling communication may be informed by old rivalries, jealousies ("Mother always loved you best," as the Smothers Brothers used to say), and unresolved—often petty—conflicts that go all the way back to childhood. By the third generation, the cousins, who may or may not know one another well, might either have absorbed a great deal of positive energy or be carrying their parents' baggage into their interactions with the family members of their own generation.

The Perils of the "Other Conversation"

Although human beings talk a lot, nonverbal communication makes up anywhere from 75 to 90 percent of our total communication efforts.[3] The lift of an eyebrow, a tiny postural change, or pursed lips can be the most telling aspects of any conversation.

Nonverbals can erect a barrier to communication even within a single culture. However, today's ultra-wealthy families often are spread out internationally, and members of a far-flung family may marry into another culture. Even if both marital partners are fluent in the language used by the family, nonverbal cultural signals can be powerful—and misunderstood. Such issues as eye contact (optics), gestures, and touch (haptics) can be misinterpreted, and the result may be unintended slights or outright insults that can gum up the entire web of communication. In a global world, knowledge of other cultural norms is essential for business purposes; for a family, such understanding is a prerequisite for unity and harmony. If the family needs help in navigating cultural barriers, the subject is a good one to learn about and discuss at a family retreat or assembly.

In spite of the potential barriers, nowhere is transparency in conversation more important than in a family as it deals with its multigenerational legacy. Daniel's family must be able to hear and understand the viewpoints represented by his cousin Noah's family, whether the cousins live across the street or across the world from one another. It can be a tricky business that sometimes requires intervention by an expert in multicultural communication.

Methods of Communication

As we examine the communication tools already mentioned—conference calls, newsletters, and quarterly reports, for example—it appears that all the communication flows from the top. That style works well if one person, such as the wealth creator, controls all the assets and decisions. However, as the family grows and control becomes decentralized, dictates from on high don't work anymore. In a group of fifty family members, there may be as many as fifty opinions about how a financial decision should be made, so despotic declarations are doomed from the start.

Communication works best when it is timely, clear, and ongoing. Modern technology makes that possible, and today's wealthy families expect information to be available at the touch of a key or a swipe across the phone. In fact, *The Futurewealth Report: Stepping into the Communication Age 2012–2013*[4] revealed that high-net and ultra-high-net-worth individuals "have a strong appetite for digital communication and ... expect their financial providers to follow suit." The report also stated that it's the richest of the rich who were the "earliest adopters ... [spending] 28 hours on digital ... communication per week, compared with 19 hours among [wealthy individuals] as a whole." Although texting and other forms of digital communication have become more prevalent, it was the "uber-wealthy" who pioneered these forms, and their appetite for them appears to have remained constant or increased over time.

In response, many wealth-management firms or groups of professionals have created dedicated, secure family portals for basic communications: net worth today, asset allocation changes, or dates of the next family meeting.

The portal also can house newsletters or other communiques about shifts in the macroeconomic environment, international investing, changes to the tax code, updates to legislation, philanthropic opportunities, and a host of other topics of interest to the family. Family members can check in anytime from anywhere. Perhaps most important, a sophisticated portal can serve as a communication hub in which family members can ask questions about what they've read or heard and receive answers either from their professional advisors, members of the communications team, or other family experts.

If immediate action is needed, families are becoming more and more comfortable with text messages. Today, busy people may check their email only every day or so, but texts create a sense of immediacy, and those receiving them tend to respond much more quickly than they would to an email. Digital natives are particularly at home with this kind of communication. Many texts can be sent at once, making them more efficient even than telephone calls. In a crisis, texts are invaluable, even if all they do is direct respondents to the family portal for immediate information, action plans, and permissions.

Messages, however they are transmitted, should reflect the family's information needs and communication preferences. Some family members don't want to spend every waking minute staring at a screen, especially if they do so all day working in the family enterprise. They prefer ink-and-paper news they can read at leisure. They like to take their time digesting the data and writing marginal notes and questions. These communiques don't have to be glossy, four-color newsletters. A simple black-and-white presentation is usually enough. Some prefer their updates to arrive on a regular schedule, whether that's daily, monthly, quarterly, semiannually, or even annually, while others like the up-to-the-minute advantages of electronic information.

Clients may want face-to-face communication, but if family members are scattered throughout the country or the world, interactive programs such as Skype or FaceTime may have to suffice, providing time zone issues can be worked out.

If electronic communication is the preferred method, today's families demand firewalls that are resistant to hacking and data breaches. A portal that isn't secure can expose family information and personal communication to the world.

For working on basal issues, such as the mission and values statements or such decisions as changing the investment strategy, choosing philanthropic directions, or preparing the next generation to assume new roles, nothing beats a high-touch, all-hands-on-deck assembly facilitated by experts who assist the family in dealing with the concerns that are the subjects of the meeting. It is a time to examine—or reexamine—the family's goals or figure out how to realign family dynamics so the mission is accomplished with a minimum of friction or stress. And when the business is done, bonding is enhanced by a variety of family activities, history sessions, and whatever the group feels is comfortable and enjoyable to do together as family units or an extended clan. It's ideal when the family leaves such gatherings or retreats with a sense of camaraderie and renewed purpose.

Who Talks?

Ideally, in a family, everyone has a chance to have the floor. Some will try to dominate all conversations. Some don't have much interest in communicating at all. As with any bell curve, though, the vast majority are in the middle. These are the constituents who want to have some sort of say in the family decision-making process, whether that's a lot of input or simply an occasional check-in.

However, it's probably members of the family council or its communication subcommittee—possibly informed by its professional advisors or family office—who will handle the majority of outgoing communication. They are, after all, the ones closest to the action, and they may have special expertise in investments, banking, or other financial disciplines.

Nonetheless, those charged with outgoing communication may not be the ones best equipped to deal with incoming messages. Communication is a balanced equation: talking and listening. Data-gatherers and tacticians may be articulate spokespersons, but they may not have the listening skills necessary to ensure clear communication.

Listening is an important but often underappreciated talent. In fact, research tells us that most people remember only about 50 percent of what they hear, and after a period of forty-eight hours, memory drops to approximately 25 percent. Good listeners up that ante:

- *They pay attention to content.* They listen to the speaker's words and focus on what's being said rather than on the speaker's style of presentation, what he or she is wearing, or counting the "ers" or "ums" the speaker drops into the conversation. Not everyone is a polished orator, but he or she may have very sound opinions and ideas.
- *They concentrate on the speaker.* No, they don't stare at them unblinkingly, which is likely to create uneasiness, but they also don't check their messages or play games on their phones, either. Nothing makes a person feel more important than been fully seen and heard.
- *They avoid rehearsal.* Good listeners don't formulate their responses while the other person is still talking. Rehearsing is the antithesis of paying attention and concentrating—and when the listener butts into the other person's narrative with a well-rehearsed answer (often a defense or rebuttal), it's a dead giveaway that he or she hasn't been listening to a word the conversational partner was saying.[5]

Listening keeps discussion moving because good listeners ask the important questions, make an attempt to involve every stakeholder in the conversation, attend to every viewpoint, and assist in finding areas of agreement, especially if those involved seem to be at opposite ends of the communication spectrum.

Excellent listeners also keep the end game in mind. Rather than be bogged down in the minutiae of a difference of opinion about how money should be disbursed or invested, an exceptional listener can develop rapport with a variety of family members and guide the conversation in a positive direction by leading them to consider what impact their personal desires may have on the family mission and values. Keeping those values at the forefront often can result in a workable compromise even if family members seem to be at an impasse.

In short, then, a communication subcommittee or handpicked members of the family council should include both great talkers and superior listeners. If listening skills are not resident in family members, more and more wealth management teams include psychologists and other professionals trained in listening and conflict resolution. As Jim Grubman, author of *Strangers in Paradise: How Families Adapt to Wealth Across Generations,* says, both family members who wish to take on an important communications role and their advisors should possess "great communication skills, the ability to listen [and] show empathy, skill in interviewing and responding to multiple family members, and even skills in speaking clearly without jargon to all types of clients."[6]

Clear, precise upstream and downstream communications are critical to family wealth management. If communication is neglected, even the most carefully planned strategies and tactics may founder—and family unity may suffer irreparable harm.

Notes

1. Mass Mutual American Family Business Survey, 2007, www.massmutual.com/mmfg/pdf/afbs.pdf. Retrieved July 25, 2016.
2. Sylvia Shepherd, "Representing Family Constituencies: The Role of the Family Council," *The Practitioner* (August 20, 2014), ffipractitioner.org/2014/08/20/representing-family-constituencies-the-role-of-the-family-council/. Retrieved July 20, 2016.
3. Gretchen Hirsch, *The Complete Idiot's Guide to Difficult Conversations* (New York: Alpha Books, 2007), p. 13.
4. "The Futurewealth Report 2012–2013: Stepping into the Communication Age," www.seic.com/ScorpioPartnership.FuturewealthPT2.USversion_Final-web.pdf. Retrieved July 27, 2016.
5. Hirsch, p. 32.
6. Gary Shunk, "Ultra-High-Net-Worth Families Are Very Different from the Simply Wealthy," CEG Worldwide LLC, www.cegworldwide.com/resources/expert-team/140-ei-shunk-grubman-ultra-high-net-worth-families. Retrieved July 21, 2016.

CHAPTER 12

Integrating Tactical Wealth Management

Because strategic wealth management is so often relegated to second-class status behind the tactics related to building and protecting a family's assets, this book has dealt largely with strategy.

This is not to say that tactical wealth management isn't a critical pursuit. A family cannot successfully manage wealth without a tactical plan because strategic wealth management, despite its importance, is not a stand-alone proposition. The true formula for increasing wealth and sustaining it over generations is the integration of tactical wealth management and strategic processes. One is not nearly as effective as both.

The order in which these two disciplines are taken up is different for every family. Some, particularly those who experience a sudden wealth event, may need to deal with immediate tactical concerns—taxation and estate planning perhaps chief among them. However, if tactics can be hung on the overarching scaffolding of solid, values-based strategy, so much the better, especially as the family grows and the generations replace one another.

The tactical issues that require placement in a strategic framework include:

- Cash flow planning, budgeting, and financial forecasting
- Banking, including credit management and money movement
- Tax planning and compliance
- Risk management and insurance planning
- Asset management and investment management
- Business management and direct investments
- Family office creation and management
- Information management and reporting

Cash Flow, Budgeting, and Financial Forecasting

If wealth has come quickly through the sale of a successful business, for example, the family may need a good deal of help to manage the cash that has been part of the sale. Although family members might have been successful at handling day-to-day or even strategic operations, those skills don't necessarily carry over to understanding the repercussions of handling huge amounts of cash.

This kind of immediate wealth, while it has upsides, also can be unsettling and cause varying degrees of anxiety. There's a name for these disconcerting feelings: sudden wealth syndrome (SWS), a term coined in an article by the Money, Meaning & Choice Institute to describe "the psychological issues . . . associated with new or sudden wealth."[1] In its description of the term, the institute names several possible signs of the syndrome:

- Anxiety and panic
- Irritability
- Guilt
- Depression
- Sleep disorders
- Paranoid thinking
- Excessive worry about every uptick and downtick in the stock market

The article goes on to say, however, that the situation can be turned around. "People with SWS can . . . re-balance themselves in the major domains of living: self, relationships, work, and community. This means making choices that align one's life with [one's] core values." In short, these people can discover, as have many before them, that wealth is about much more than money. It's about making money work to accomplish important family and legacy goals.

Not every person who comes into wealth in a hurry falls apart, but for those who are having trouble dealing with the consequences of an influx of money, psychological counseling can be invaluable—and for nearly everyone in this situation, financial counseling is a must.

A qualified financial advisor or financial planner will be important in building a program that helps the family develop budgets, manage cash flow and cash requirements, and create financial forecasts. These professionals can work with the family to answer key questions such as:

- What is the best thing to do with the cash now?
- What are our immediate cash demands?

- What are our short- and long-term capital requirements?
- How much cash does the family need in short-term liquid instruments as an emergency or opportunity fund?
- What other expenses will the family incur?
- What levels of income will each family member receive? Are those levels high enough?
- Does each family member have an income and expense budget?
- What types of investments are worthy of our support?
- Are there sectors we wish to avoid?
- How do we diversify our holdings for safety and growth?
- What do we see as the family dream? What matters to us individually and as a group?
- How will we use our assets to achieve the family dream?

All of these tactical questions are complex but crucial to family success and wealth sustainability. However, having to deal with them as a family without the strategic underpinning provided by vision and mission statements, constitution, and bylaws is much harder.

For families who have had wealth and wealth managers for generations, the road may be clearer. Perhaps the family has developed a cogent rationale for decision making. They may have discussed the implications of great wealth with the next generations and prepared them well to take their places in the family enterprise, whatever that may be. The family council, family meetings, and family legacy may be deeply ingrained. This is not true of *all* multigenerational families of wealth, but is becoming truer in the era of the Giving Pledge, family foundations, impact investing, and a heightened interest in philanthropy.

Those for whom wealth is a new thing will need to start from scratch, dealing as rapidly as possible with the tactical issues that must be addressed and working hard with the rest of the family to generate the strategic structure that will guide future decisions. If you think your growing business may someday result in riches, the time to prepare is today.

Banking

Unless an ultra-wealthy family is also highly sophisticated about the ins and outs of banking and credit (and some are), they likely are not optimizing their results. The large majority of families of significant means qualify for enhanced banking services often referred to as *private banking*. These individuals and families can tap into a plethora of banking or concierge services, far in excess of those offered to clients of lesser means. Some of the banking opportunities that will be useful to these families include:

- Money movement, cash processing, wire transfers, foreign exchange, and bill-payment services
- Short- and long-term lines of credit and loans
- Credit and debit cards for family members
- Reporting on transaction processing and cash balances
- E-vault capabilities to store important family documents

To determine what banking requirements the family needs, they should consider the following questions:

- Should we work with one or two banks as a group, or should we all select separate banks based on individual needs and preferences?
- What banking services will we require as individuals and as a family group?
- Should we use bank-based advisory services exclusively, or are we better served by a corps of independent advisors—or both?
- Are the fees charged by the bank's private banking service competitive with others that may offer similar products?
- Are we being encouraged to purchase certain products the bank provides because those products generate additional fee income, or do we have latitude to select what we want from among a range of services and products?
- Should we separate our various wealth management services, or is it more efficient to keep all the aspects of our wealth under one umbrella? What are the risks and benefits of each approach?
- Should we allow a bank to serve as a corporate trustee for one or more family trusts? Why or why not?

It's essential to have these questions answered, because one bad banking or money management decision can cascade and have severe deleterious effects on the family's financial health and desired legacy.

Tax Planning and Compliance

Taxes—levied by local, state, federal, and overseas jurisdictions—are a morass of mind-bending regulations, some of which seem to be at odds with one another. Tax laws can be complex, poorly worded, and confusing. They can also turn on a dime. What was a good tax strategy three years ago may have been legislated away last year. The upshot of all this incomprehensibility is that even an innocent mistake or misunderstanding of a rule can cost millions.

Because of their complicated holdings, families with significant wealth have to navigate interconnected snares of tax policy, and it's something no family should try to do on its own.

Tax planning is, of course, an ongoing activity and involves searching for as many legal ways as possible to reduce the family's tax burden. It requires the advisor to have intimate knowledge of the intricacies of tax law and the family's financial status, both now and prospectively. Filings themselves can take place at various times of the year, but planning should never wait until tax time. For greatest tax savings, families must take advantage of tax-reduction strategies far in advance of the filing date. "What you could have done in October or November to minimize your taxes may no longer be an option in March or April," said Rob Yeend.[2] "When [you file], you are reporting on what happened . . . the previous year. In the fall, you can still affect the facts of the current tax year." Missing the opportunity for a particular tax break can cost hundreds of thousands of dollars—or perhaps even more.

Unless they are properly advised, wealthy individuals and families may face special tax burdens:

- Deductions enjoyed by less-affluent taxpayers (mortgage interest, a healthy percentage of charitable contributions, real estate, state income taxes, and itemized deductions) disappear if the family's adjusted gross income exceeds a specified amount. This threshold will be crossed easily by any high-net-to ultra-high-net-worth family.
- If estate planning is not carefully executed, precious assets might have to be sold to cover estate taxes. Remember the Robbie family mentioned in Chapter 1? It's a sad story of estate planning gone wrong.
- Wealthy families also may pay higher Medicare taxes on both earned and investment income.
- Off-shore investments can result in special attention from the IRS and from the country in which the money was earned. In most cases, off-shore investment is a legitimate activity, beneficial to both the investor and the other country, but because the practice sometimes has been abused, wealthy families must be assured that all paperwork is accurate and all transactions carefully documented.
- Philanthropy, while encouraged, may have complicated reporting requirements, depending on the types of assets that are donated. Your tax advisor must be cognizant of the appraisals and forms required to make substantial charitable contributions, or the family can lose the tax benefit.

Given these considerations, it's appropriate for families to think about ways to reduce their tax obligations. The tax-reduction tactics might include important legal entity choices such as trusts, family partnerships, corporations, or foundations. Whatever a family chooses to do should be done with fore-thought about the tax ramifications, both now and in the future.

With regard to taxes, the most important thing the family can do is to work with a qualified team of tax advisors and consultants. For families with significant resources, this team typically includes, at a minimum, a tax and estate planning attorney for complex planning and entity formation and a qualified CPA to manage ongoing tax compliance and reporting. In addition, a private bank or a multifamily office can be very helpful in vetting tax strategies based on a "what-if" cost/benefit analysis.

As an aside, it's more common for those who report more than $1 million in income to be audited and even more likely for those who report more than $10 million. In 2014, less than 1 percent of all returns were audited. However, 6.21 percent of taxpayers who reported $1 million to $5 million were subject to audit, and 16 percent of those who reported more than $10 million said hello to the auditor. Overly large estate tax and international returns also may receive more attention.[3]

Risk Management

Although every aspect of life involves some degree of risk, many wealthy families and their advisors believe that risk management applies primarily to the family's investments. This is not the case; risk abounds throughout the entire wealth management process, but certainly investment risks must be managed. To do it well, the advisory group must have a thorough understanding of such investment factors as price volatility, variance drain, idiosyncratic decision making, venture capitalism, and the family's event horizons,[4] to name a few. It's about more than the price of a particular stock or group of stocks on particular day. Excellent risk management is about consistently maximizing gain and minimizing loss, and it may take more than one advisor to identify and eliminate—or at least ameliorate—the sources and effects of risk.

Since the Great Recession of 2008, many investors are rethinking these issues surrounding investment risk. David Craig, the CIO for a multifamily office, quoted in an article for *Financial Times*, said, "Wealthy families are not immune and their wealth faces some of the same threats as others."[5] Even very competent family members may find they need help in sorting out unforeseen areas of risk. The recession threw into high relief what those risks were all about. As Lauren Foster wrote, "While private clients generally understand the relationship between risk and return, many of the sophisticated financial instruments they invested in were so complex that the risks were not always obvious."[6] It was an expensive lesson for those who found that their wealth preservation and transfer plans had been upended or at least undercut.

As markets have revived since the recession, some may be investing more boldly again, but there is a greater appreciation for the risks involved—and a greater insistence that financial advisors fully inform their clients of these areas of risk. Ironically, the very wealthiest families saw some increase in the value of their holdings while the markets were diving. However, those gains certainly were not realized by every wealthy family.

Risk is not always related solely to equities. Other more tangible assets may also be at considerable risk. As Parker Beauchamp noted, "Risk factors and lifestyles increase in complexity proportionally with wealth and fame."[7] The risks might include the loss of reputation from even a frivolous lawsuit that follows the revelation of a family's net worth. A lack of appreciation for risk is evident in a feeling of invulnerability that results in unbridled spending. The continual outlay of money for houses on several continents, with their accompanying furnishings and staff; cars, planes and yachts and their crews; luxury apparel, priceless jewelry, and irreplaceable art collections can eventually drain the family fortune, even if it's immense. As the wealth creator's lifestyle gobbles up the family's financial rewards, the assets can disappear before they are passed down even to one succeeding generation.

Stephen R. Bitterman amplifies these concerns, citing three insurance deficiencies common to the affluent cohorts of society:

- They have too many brokers and too many companies managing too many policies; no entity has a comprehensive view of all the layers of risk.
- They are underinsured, sometimes to the tune of several million dollars. Because ultra-high-net-worth clients have vast holdings, the loss of which results in huge claims, standard insurance policies usually will not suffice— and it can be hard to find the policies that might fully protect all their assets.
- They don't pay enough attention to techniques and technology—especially those related "to home security, family safety, and natural disasters"—that might prevent or mitigate risks.[8]

In an earlier article, Beauchamp made the point that the more families have, the more they have to lose. He states that risk management is an integral part of the entire wealth management strategy because it "safeguards who can touch client assets, shields the wealth . . . and holds those who handle client assets accountable."[9]

In spite of the concern for risks related to investments, risk is also part of virtually every family enterprise decision.

In its report, *The State of the Art in Family Wealth Management*, the Family Office Exchange takes a broad view of risk and makes the point that all risks are not investment related, saying that "the world has become a more interconnected place in which all families are impacted by systemic risks. Therefore, families must be prepared to face more external threats and unforeseen circumstances, and they must have the awareness and flexibility to identify and seize new opportunities."[10]

For example, is all the family recordkeeping secure? What plans have been made to mitigate cyberattack, theft and publication of private information, or loss of records as a result of a natural disaster?

And speaking of natural disasters, does the family have a plan to keep the business going in a catastrophic event? How long would it take to get up and running again? How long can the family sustain the business if a return to full functioning is delayed for a protracted period of time?

Hiring can be fraught with risks. Are the family's human resources policies congruent with current law? What actions does the family take if an officer is hit with multiple sexual harassment claims? How does it handle the public relations fallout from the series of suits that follows and a negative social media campaign?

What about family malfeasance? How does the family cope with losses and uproar if one or more family members is found to be deceiving the rest about the uses of their funds?

Is the family following its own governance rules, or has governance become slapdash and casual? What effect is that having on the family enterprise, the wealth, and the legacy? How can the family remedy the situation, and what are the inherent risks if it doesn't?

A comprehensive risk management program that assesses the entire landscape of risk possibilities is a necessary part of the wealth strategy and the tactics that undergird it.

Asset and Investment Management

From the previous discussion, it's obvious that the wealthiest families need—and may have—a multitude of advisors. However, if the advisors are not part of a coordinated team with someone overseeing the group, asset management can become a quagmire. It's critical that family council members who are entrusted with understanding the asset picture work cooperatively and continually with those who are overseeing this part of the wealth.

According to a 2016 DarcMatter article reporting on a survey from the World Wealth Report 2015, American high-net-worth investors bought into the following investment instruments:

- Equities—33.9%
- Cash and cash equivalents—23.7%

- Real estate—12.3%
- Fixed income—18%
- Alternative investments—12.2%[11]

Each of these instruments has risks and benefits, and the family's portfolio requires careful coordination, balance, and expert advice related to asset allocation. In fact, asset allocation is seen by many as the bedrock on which all wealth management decisions rest. An out-of-balance portfolio may result in unacceptable risk, and unacceptable—and perhaps unknown—risk may trigger large losses. For some extraordinarily wealthy families, a loss may be an inconvenience, but even for ultra-high-net-worth families, a significant loss can have a major impact on the family's coherence and legacy. When it comes to assets and asset allocation—and even where the assets are located—families need to ask themselves some questions:

- Do we have an overly concentrated position in the stock in our own company or the one who bought our business? What do we do about that?
- Are we overly concentrated in any other sector, such as pharmaceuticals or energy? How should we rebalance our portfolio, when, and what will it cost?
- How much liquidity does the family need? Are we tying up too much of what we have in assets that are hard to liquidate if we have to?
- Have we aligned our asset allocation and asset location with the purpose behind each investment? Do we have a clear, shared understanding of the goals of each family member and the family overall? Does the overall investment plan support these objectives?
- If we have invested offshore, how safe are those investments today? Has any governmental or system change made the investments more risky? Who's watching that situation carefully?
- What is our investment style? Active or passive? Quick growth or longer-term investment? How risk-averse is the family? What kinds of equities are most attractive to us? Small up-and-comers or well-established companies with recognizable brands? Do our advisors understand and act on our preferences and tolerance for risk when making investment decisions with us?
- For each investment pool, have we developed a written investment policy that defines investment objectives, risk tolerances, asset allocation guidelines, decision-making processes, return expectations, preferences, and restrictions? Have we shared that investment policy with all of our investment advisors and other members of our wealth management team?
- What are the potential downsides of alternative investments such as commodities, hedge funds, venture capital, and precious metals? Are we comfortable in that space?

- Are our advisors equally expert in every type of investment? If not, what other help do we need?
- We are interested in learning more about investment generally so we can work with our advisory team more effectively. How much interest do our investment advisors have in educating us? Where else can we receive more information?

An emerging area of asset management is impact investing. Currently, wealthy families are becoming more interested in making these types of investments. "The growing impact investment market provides capital to address the world's most pressing challenges in sectors such as sustainable agriculture, clean technology, microfinance, and affordable and accessible basic services including housing, healthcare, and education," says the Global Impact Investing Network.[12] These investments are not philanthropy; in almost all cases, a return is expected. Investors do not own or manage the company, so impact investment might be termed a cousin of direct investment. It's an avenue a family can take to effect social and environmental change.

Business Management and Direct Investment

As several of the case studies in this book demonstrate, many wealthy people find that simply managing their wealth, traveling, or engaging in hobbies is insufficient for them to feel connected in their lives. They want something more. Some establish family foundations and immerse themselves in philanthropy or specific causes. Others, still fascinated by business, want to invest directly in either operating companies or real estate projects. They don't want to just plunk down cash, however. They want to be involved. Direct investment gives them the opportunity to invest in companies or projects in which they can be in control, make a difference, and find a sense of purpose.

In a direct investment scenario, the family buys operating companies or real property and manages those assets directly. Effectively, it means the individual family members or the family as a whole owns and manages the company they invest in. Perhaps it is a venture investment into a new or emerging business opportunity or a company that is struggling. Regardless of the type of entity, the family feels that with their intervention, business acumen, and cash infusion, they can have direct control and earn a higher rate of return on their assets than may be available in the public markets. However, often these types of investments are long-term and hard to sell quickly, so it is important that families stay diversified and not be overly concentrated in direct investments or other illiquid assets.

Whether a family is a business-owing family, has become a financial family after a liquidity event, or is buying into new ventures, management tasks go on, and they may become even more burdensome as the family increases in size and complexity. Business management experts can work with the family's advisors to analyze their current and projected financial status and carry out the tactical tasks that must be accomplished to help the family reach its highest goals.

Family Office Creation and Management

As discussed in Chapter 5, single-family offices (SFOs) are for the top-of-the-pole wealthy. A single-family office is run and managed for the benefit of one family. They own it, they control it, and they don't share services with anyone else. It's easier for the family to maintain confidentiality and privacy about sensitive matters because the office is run by trusted advisors and family members who work only for the family. The costs, however, are usually in the neighborhood of $1 million per year, and most clients have at least $500 million to $1 billion in investable assets.

If a family cannot afford a single-family office, the multifamily office (MFO) provides a way for several families to receive a full gamut of services at a lesser price. MFOs are one of the fastest-growing sectors in financial services. "The genesis of the new multifamily offices is coming from . . . accounting firms, financial planning firms, registered investment advisors, spin-off teams from private bank and broker-dealer wealth management platforms [and] spin-off teams from investment management firms," said Linda Mack.[13] To be a true family office, the firm must offer:

- Integrated tax and estate planning
- Investment strategy
- Trusteeship
- Risk management
- Lifestyle management
- Recordkeeping and reporting
- Family continuity
- Family philanthropy[14]

It's important, then, when seeking to become part of such a group to question the advisors carefully and to unearth all the services they provide. Questions might include:

- How experienced is each advisor, and what is the depth of experience of the entire office?

- Are there recognized specialists who can deal with any of our family's unique situations?
- What are your affiliations with other firms that provide products and services for families like ours? Are your recommendations for our family affected by any financial considerations related to these relationships?
- Will there be a specific person who will serve as the nerve center and point of contact for our family?
- Who will handle the day-to-day tasks such as recordkeeping and tax compliance?
- Prior to our making a decision, may we interview each member of the firm who would be dealing with our family?
- Are there additional services, such as travel planning and purchase advice on large-ticket items, such as new aircraft, that we can tap into as members of this office?
- How are costs assessed? Are there any hidden expenses we should know about now?
- What checks and balances does the firm have in place to ensure that there are no mistakes based on dishonesty, incompetence, or preventable errors? Can we feel safe that all your advisors meet the highest personal and professional standards?

Information Management and Reporting

Financial performance is dependent on reliable information, but families of significant wealth may have a large pool of diverse assets held in different locations and managed by a variety of advisors. These families need a timely, unified view of their assets. Without such a 360-degree outlook, the family has a more difficult time administering its own wealth and the legacy it wishes to establish for current and future generations.

Measuring and reporting critical goal-driven data are important keys to successful decision making and long-term wealth management. After all, if you don't know where you are, how will you get to where you want to be? Below are some important questions to ask your wealth advisors:

- How often will I receive performance reports?
- In what form will my reports arrive?
- Will my reports aggregate and consolidate data from my entire wealth picture or just from my equity investments?
- Can you generate customized reports such as net worth statements for the family and its branches?
- How often do you create comprehensive financial reports? Yearly? Monthly? As we request?

- If there is a sudden national or international event that has an impact on our family wealth picture, how quickly can you report the effects of that event on our plans? How will that information come to us? Will you simply report it, or will you make immediate recommendations?
- How reliable and secure is your current information management and reporting technology?
- How rapidly do you take advantage of new and better technology?
- What kinds of specialists do you have managing that technology?
- Do we have 24/7 digital access to important data?
- While we like digital access for certain tasks, we like to discuss certain things, such as long-term planning and investment strategies, face-to-face. Are both ways of doing business equally important to you or do you rely primarily on online interactions?

Winding Up

As is evident from the lists of questions above, tactical wealth management is a complicated, interlocking web of decisions. With the help of advisors, the family may make highly successful tactical decisions. It may prosper, but prosperity today doesn't guarantee prosperity tomorrow. Wealth is more than piling up assets for today. The power of wealth resides in how a family uses it and passes it on over a long period of time. Having a strategic plan in place makes all tactical decisions clearer and more defensible. The family is more likely to sustain its wealth, rather than squandering it by the third generation, by maintaining a unified, strategic posture regarding the growth and use of the family fortune.

Obviously, a critical component in integrating the tactical and strategic aspects of effective long-term wealth management is selecting, coordinating, and overseeing the nonfamily service providers and the professional advisory teams that should be an important part of the process. These teams will include attorneys, accountants and other tax experts, bankers, investment managers and consultants, insurance specialists versed in complex risks, family succession planning advisors, estate planners, and unaffiliated family employees and board members. This coordination effort is enhanced when families have developed and continue to refine their strategic plans as a tool to improve the performance and effectiveness of their tactical procedures.

In the following—and last—chapter of this book is a case study of the Singleton family, whose strategic and tactical plans have meshed, providing the families with financial growth, unity, exceptional wealth management, and a legacy that will live for generations to come.

Notes

1. "Sudden Wealth Syndrome," Money, Meaning & Choices Institute (2010), www.mmcinstitute.com/about-2/sudden-wealth-syndrome. Retrieved September 7, 2016.
2. Rob Yeend, "Tax Minimization: Planning vs. Compliance," Brammer and Yeend (October 9, 2015), http://brammerandyeend.com/tax-minimization-planning-vs-compliance/?doing_wp_cron=1482503818.2447090148925781250000. Retrieved September 10, 2016.
3. Karen Brandeisky, "These Are the People Who Are Most Likely to Get Audited," Money (April 14, 2015), time.com/money/3820009/irs-tax-audit-chances. Retrieved September 11, 2016.
4. An excellent discussion of these issues can be found in Gregory Curtis's book, The Stewardship of Wealth: Successful Private Wealth Management for Investors and Their Advisors (Hoboken, NJ: John Wiley & Sons, 2013), pp. 73–97.
5. Lauren Foster, "High Net Worth Clients Rethink Concept of Risk," Financial Times (January 12, 2009), www.ft.com/content/9756968a-e103-11dd-b0e8-00 0077b07658. Retrieved September 12, 2016.
6. Ibid.
7. Parker Beauchamp, "Are You Protecting Your High-Net-Worth Clients from Risk?" WealthManagement.com (June 23, 2015), wealthmanagement.com/client-relations/are-you-protecting-your-high-net-worth-clients-risk. Retrieved September 8, 2015.
8. Stephen Bitterman, "What Are the Special Insurance Needs of Individuals Worth $10 or More?" Northington Insurance Group, LLC (August/September 2013), www.northingtonllc.com/Wort_Steve_Bitterman_7_2013.pdf. Retrieved September 10, 2016.
9. Parker Beauchamp, "Why Risk Management Belongs in Your Client's Portfolio," Wealthmanagement.com (January 7, 2015), wealthmanagement.com/high-net-worth/why-risk-management-belongs-your-client-s-portfolio. Retrieved September 12, 2016.
10. "The State of the Art in Family Wealth Management: 2013–2014 FOX Thought Leaders Council Summit Report," www.familyoffice.com/knowledge-center/state-art-family-wealth-management. Retrieved September 27, 2016.
11. DarcMatter Blog; "What Do the Wealthy Invest Their Money In?" blog entry by Grace Kim, January 20, 2016, blog.darcmatter.com/what-do-the-wealthy-invest-their-money-in. Retrieved September 12, 2016.
12. "What You Need to Know About Impact Investing," Global Impact Investing Network, thegiin.org/impact-investing/need-to-know/#s1. Retrieved September 14, 2016.
13. Russ Alan Prince, "The Multi-Family Office Gold Rush," Forbes (November 12, 2013), www.forbes.com/sites/russalanprince/2013/11/12/the-multi-family-office-gold-rush/#218c2bc47d38m, November 12, 2013. Retrieved September 13, 2016.
14. Sara Hamilton, "Multi-Family Office Mania," WealthManagement.com (December 19, 2002), wealthmanagement.com/news/multi-family-office-mania-0. Retrieved September 13, 2016.

CHAPTER 13

Getting It Right

As Dr. David Singleton* entered Donovan's Restaurant, just as he had done many times before over the last twenty-seven years, he was overcome with a wave of emotion. He realized this was among many traditions that were about to change. After almost every board meeting for the last ten years, he, the Biocellular Health Sciences* board, and his senior leadership team met to share dinner. Tonight, this meal would be different because the purpose was to celebrate his retirement, although it was strange for him to think of this evening as a celebration.

Walking through the restaurant, he soaked in the smells, the sounds, and the décor to imprint them in his memory like a permanent photograph. His mind drifted back to the day he interviewed for his first research position with Doring Pharmaceuticals* after finishing his fellowship at Stanford. That day was the first time he had lunch at Donovan's. It felt like a lifetime ago and, in many ways, it was.

David had served as CEO of Biocellular for the last decade, over-seeing its becoming one of the dominant biomedical firms in the world. He led the company's development of industry-leading therapies and medications that were helping to provide cures for several forms of cancer, and the company now was venturing into ground-breaking research on dementia. His industry reputation as an innovator, collaborator, and leader distinguished him as an industry icon. Throughout his tenure, Biocellular had grown to be one of the most valuable life science companies in the world, with the stock price increasing by 260 percent over the last seven years.

---

*The examples with an asterisk mentioned in this chapter are composites of cases the author has encountered in his wealth management career. Names and all identifying details have been changed to protect privacy.

145

In addition, although he never thought of himself in this way, he had become a very wealthy man, accumulating in excess of $300 million in Biocellular stock. He did not feel particularly "rich," because in the previous twenty-seven years he had never sold a share of his stock in the company.

In fact, he, his wife, Elaine,* and their four children lived a very modest lifestyle given the extent of their wealth. David and Elaine still lived in the same four-bedroom house they scraped the funds together to purchase nineteen years ago after their youngest child, Gretchen,* was born. Now, with Gretchen off to college, all four kids—Tom,* Stacy,* Trevor,* and Gretchen—were effectively living independently, forging their paths and building their own futures. The two oldest, Tom and Stacy, were married and each had two children of their own.

For this last official dinner with his team and the board, Elaine, all four kids, and Tom's and Stacy's spouses, Wendy* and Peter,* were joining the group to share in the recognition of David's contributions during his tenure at Biocellular. During and after dinner, there was a lot of laughter, a few tears, and tremendous feelings of warmth and some degree of melancholy from everyone in the room. David was overwhelmed and overcome with sentiment from the tremendous love emanating from all the tables that night.

The next day was David's last official day on the job. Dr. Stuart Cooper* would be taking over as the new CEO and chair of the board. David felt strongly that he wanted to make a clean break and let Stuart, his mentee and friend, start down the path of building his vision for next stage of the company. Now the big question on David's mind, and, in fact, on everyone else's, including his family's, was what he would do next.

That day, as he sat for the last time in the corner office on the seventeenth floor of Biocellular's headquarters, he knew that transitioning to the next stage of life was not going to be easy for him. There were a host of things to consider and decisions to be made. His life was about to change in ways he could not even imagine. He decided to put those considerations out of his mind so he could be present for his last day as the company leader.

Facing the Future: Transition from a Business Executive to Running a Financial Enterprise

Two weeks after his last day at work and after spending time with Elaine, the kids, and the grandchildren on Martha's Vineyard, David came home to an empty house. The first morning after breakfast, Elaine went off to her yoga class and then to a charity luncheon for a local art museum. As he made his way into the office they had converted from Stacy's room when she went to college, David had his first time truly alone to consider the future.

He sat down at his desk with a blank pad of paper and the beautiful fountain pen he received as one of his gifts from the Biocellular board. He looked at the paper and the paper looked at him. Neither one spoke to the other. After a few minutes, he wrote down four words:

- Family
- Passion
- Impact
- Legacy

He didn't really know why those words ended up on paper. After a bit more thought, however, he realized they had come to him as he was thinking about what was most important to him in life. He had so many things to consider, decisions to make, and opportunities to contemplate. He wondered what he should do first, so he put on his CEO hat and began to prioritize.

Now that he was no longer employed by the company, he recognized that he needed to make some important immediate financial decisions:

- What should he do about the company pension plan?
- How should he handle his stock options and restricted stock?
- Would he need to review all of his insurance to make sure he has the proper coverage as a retiree?
- How should he pay his bills and cover his expenses now that he would no longer receive a regular paycheck?

He decided that the next step to get the process moving was to assemble a team of his key advisors and bring them together for a meeting. He started by calling his attorney, Stan White.* Stan had been his attorney and friend for twenty years. Along with Stan, he called his accountant, Randall Turnberry,* and his investment advisor, Jeffrey Renwick.* He asked them to join him and Elaine for a meeting on Thursday of the following week at Stan's office.

David and Elaine arrived at Stan's at 9:45 A.M. The meeting was scheduled for 10 A.M. Elaine told David she was a bit nervous and uncomfortable. She did not particularly like dealing with financial and legal issues, and she was a little tense that she would be the only woman in the room. She told David that Jeffrey, in particular, sometimes talked down to her and seemed somewhat condescending and patronizing. David was surprised to hear that, and he told her that he would observe Jeffrey during the meeting.

As they walked into the plush conference room in Stan's office, all of the invited participants were already there. David and Elaine greeted the team warmly and after a few pleasantries, everyone sat down at the large mahogany conference table. David stated that he would like to address the group. He said, "As you all know, I just retired from Biocellular after twenty-seven years. Spending the majority of my professional life at such a wonderful company was an immense pleasure and an honor. I loved it up to my very last day, but it is now time for me and Elaine to build the next chapter in our lives. I am not exactly sure yet what it will look like. However, I'm excited to enter the future.

"As you are all aware, we have been very fortunate due to Biocellular's success and generosity. We've been able to accumulate a substantial level of financial resources. In fact, it is more than I could ever have imagined we would have and far more than we will ever need.

"The first purpose of our meeting today is to make some necessary, important, and timely financial, legal, and tax decisions. Elaine and I will need all of your help to address these issues. However, over the last few days and weeks, I have begun to feel the immense opportunity and responsibility that our wealth carries. We will never spend what we have.

"We need to consider the bigger picture of what this wealth means to us and how we want to deploy it most effectively. This part of the process will take time and effort, and I will be looking to all of you, my family, and others to participate in helping us build a plan for the future."

He then asked Elaine if she would like to say anything. She said, "I am so very proud of David and all he has accomplished. I know that leaving Biocellular and retiring was one of the most profound and difficult decisions he has ever made—and he has made a lot of tough decisions. The most important thing to me is that the next stage of our lives has as much meaning and fulfillment as the last one."

After David and Elaine were finished, all of the advisors in the room were a bit stunned and speechless. It was rare to hear clients have such a thoughtful approach to how they viewed their wealth. After a good thirty seconds of silence, which felt like a long time, someone finally spoke. Stan jumped in and said, "David and Elaine, you have been my clients and my friends for a long time. I am extremely touched and proud, as we all are, to have been selected to help you and your family with this journey.

"You have my commitment that we will work diligently and collaboratively to help you build a plan that will achieve the results you are looking for." Jeffrey and Randall chimed in and stated they were similarly committed to being part of the team to build the right plan for the Singleton family.

For the rest of the meeting, the group discussed the immediate short-term steps David needed to take with regard to some of the pertinent time-sensitive financial issues. After leaving the meeting, Elaine told David she liked Stan and Randall, but was not sure that Jeffrey was the right person to help them with their investments and other financial affairs. David agreed and told Elaine he would meet with Stan and ask for some referrals to other advisors.

The following week, David had the private meeting with Stan. He told Stan that he and Elaine were excited to have Stan and Randall on their advisory team. However, he did not feel that Jeffrey had the comprehensive wealth management knowledge or investment expertise to support the family's needs as they enter this next stage.

"Jeffery is a really nice guy," David said, "and he's been helpful and effective in managing a few million dollars we've entrusted to him over the last several years, but we feel we need a much different level of wealth management capabilities than what he and his firm can offer. Both Elaine and I take very seriously the responsibility of managing and stewarding our assets as effectively as we possibly can. We want them to make a meaningful impact on the people and things we care about. We need advisors who can help us achieve this outcome."

"I understand your perspective about Jeffrey," Stan replied, "and I tend to agree with it. He is a quality advisor and an ethical professional, but I don't believe he's the right person or represents the best firm to meet your new requirements. I'm actually glad you brought it up because I have been thinking about your goals, and I do have a recommendation for you.

"I recently worked with another family that was going through a similar wealth transition," Stan went on. "They had many of the same objectives and concerns you do. I introduced them to Rebecca George* at Legacy Wealth Collaborators.* Her firm takes a qualitative and quantitative approach to helping families manage wealth. They're familiar with the issues and opportunities facing wealthy families like yours. Rebecca has been working with the family I referred to her for over a year, and they have made tremendous progress in their wealth management. They're delighted with her. I suggest we arrange a meeting with her so you can learn more about how they can support your family."

Two weeks later, David and Elaine meet with Stan and Rebecca George. As David and Elaine became acquainted with Rebecca, they both found her warm and approachable, with a healthy degree of natural curiosity. She asked insightful questions that demonstrated her experience in working with several families in similar circumstances to the Singletons. That experience gave her credibility with the couple.

After learning more about them, Rebecca explained how her firm worked with families like theirs. She told them that LWC focused on what she referred to as both the strategic and tactical aspects of wealth management, so that families of significant resources could be successful in working with the assets they controlled and the impact those assets might have on the things that mattered to the Singletons. She went on to explain that long-term, effective wealth management is difficult and fails more often than it succeeds for most families. She detailed the fact that the high percentage of failures came from a lack of focus on the strategic issues such as family harmony, communication, role clarity, family education, and preparation of the succeeding generations. She said the key to successful, sustainable wealth management was the integration of both strategic and tactical planning and explained that LWC delivered its services through the efforts of a multidisciplinary team who designed a planning process that treated the business of family as a family enterprise.

David and Elaine were both impressed. What they were hearing was very different from what they had experienced before, and it was perfectly aligned with what they were looking for. They asked several questions about fees, specific services, and how the process would work for their family. Rebecca said that if they were interested in moving forward, the first step would be a meeting to understand their specific priorities and their goals. After that meeting, she would develop a scope of engagement document that would define the services, timeline, and outcomes for their review and consideration.

A couple weeks later, David and Elaine met with Rebecca and a few of her partners at the LWC offices. Their current advisors, Stan and Randall, participated as well. During the meeting, Rebecca and Stan asked David and Elaine a great deal more about their current situation and their quantitative and qualitative planning requirements and objectives.

Some of the key quantitative issues included:

- The couple's current balance sheet, their income requirements, and their current and future anticipated income estimates
- The anticipated income requirements of any other family members or dependents they supported
- Their current investment portfolio, including holdings, asset allocation, risk tolerance, and investment objectives
- David's employee benefits and company retirement plan
- The status of their holdings in Biocellular stock
- Their current and future income, gift, and estate tax scenario
- Their current estate plan and estate planning objectives

The qualitative areas covered topics such as:

- Their thoughts about how they wanted to spend their time currently and in the future
- Their current values and passions
- How much communication they had done with their children about their wealth
- The level of wealth they wanted their family members to receive

- What other issues were important to them in regard to impact with their resources
- The children and grandchildren's level of preparation to receive and manage a significant amount of wealth
- The roles they wanted family members and others to play in the management of their resources

The session went on for more than two hours, and by the end, David and Elaine were tired but also highly stimulated and engaged. For the first time, David began to connect directly with the opportunity and the magnitude of the impact that their resources could provide. He was in the beginning of transitioning his mindset from CEO of a business enterprise to CEO of a family enterprise.

Although they made significant progress in defining their priorities, goals, and objectives, many unresolved issues were still on the table. David and Elaine needed time to process some of the important questions that they had never contemplated before.

Rebecca suggested that they get together again in a couple weeks to further define their goals and requirements. She offered to summarize the areas they needed to deliberate in a memo for them.

A few weeks later, the group met again for another session. Prior to the meeting, David and Elaine spent several hours connecting and getting on the same page about some of the key questions and unresolved issues. Their preparation helped focus and streamline the discussion. At the end of the second session, Rebecca said that she would take what she had learned and develop an engagement proposal that would summarize the couple's current situation, their goals and objectives, and how LWC would suggest working with them and their other advisors.

The following week, Rebecca sent an engagement proposal to Stan and Randall to review before it went to the Singletons. The document outlined the primary goals and requirements the group had discussed during their prior meetings. In addition, she put the action items into three areas: short-term tactical requirements; long-term strategy development and implementation; and long-term tactical requirements and implementation.

Short-Term Tactical Requirements: Singleton Family

- Develop an income and expense budget and forecast for Elaine and David.
- Review the Biocellular pension plan options and employee benefits to determine what elections need to be made and identify any gaps in coverage.
- Develop a plan for starting to diversify out of Biocellular stock, including the structuring of a noncorrelated investment portfolio to Biocellular stock.

- Create a current and future income tax forecast for David and Elaine.
- Review the Singletons' current estate plan to determine if it is adequate as a short-term, gap strategy.

Long-Term Strategy Development and Implementation: Singleton Family

- Create a family vision and mission statement for the management of the wealth as an enterprise.
- Develop a family communication plan to share the appropriate details that David and Elaine want their family members to know.
- Determine how David and Elaine want to allocate their wealth over the long term between their family members and the private foundation they plan to create.
- Define and develop the focus of the foundation around the areas of impact that matter to David, Elaine, and the rest of the Singleton family.
- Determine what roles and responsibilities are required to run the family enterprise and define the participation of family members.
- Develop and implement an ongoing family wealth educational program.

Long-Term Tactical Requirements and Implementation: Singleton Family

- Implement and provide for an annual family retreat focused on stewardship and education.
- Complete the process for distributing assets to each of the children and grandchildren so that each child has $10 million and each grandchild receives $1 million.
- Develop and implement the Singleton Family Investment Partnership focused on direct and venture investments. Determine the roles of each family member.
- Develop and implement the Singleton Family Foundation in regard to the mission, management, and administration. Determine the roles of each family member.
- Complete David and Elaine's long-term estate plan and communicate it to the children.
- Set up additional support for managing the wealth and the foundation on behalf of the family.

The New World: The Singleton Family Enterprise Two Years Later

It is 8:30 Tuesday morning, and David and Elaine's oldest son, Tom, is making his way up the stairs of the three-floor townhouse David purchased six months ago. This area of town is still going through some gentrification, but David loved the building and wanted to be "where the action is." Renovation of the third floor recently was completed, and Singleton Ventures, LLC, and the Singleton Family Foundation now occupy five offices, a conference room, and a multiuse common area where David added a pool table because he thought it would make his grandchildren see that he really was cool.

Today is an important day because the family is meeting with Dr. Tony Delmetro,* head of research at University Hospital, to finalize a grant for establishing the Singleton Center for Pediatric Cancer Research. The hospital already has raised more than $30 million, and David and his family have committed to an initial funding of $11.5 million through the Singleton Foundation. Given his career in cancer research and Elaine's interest in bettering children's lives, they are very excited about this project.

Tom knows that David has been in the office since 7:00 A.M. per his normal routine. As Tom makes his way to the top of stairs, he is reminded how much his dad has changed since his retirement from Biocellular. He cannot even remember what David looked like in a suit, since his dad has not worn one in almost two years; the last time was to a wedding, and he complained about it. His daily wardrobe is usually a pair of denim jeans and a golf shirt.

It is clear to all the members of his family and his friends that David is completely engaged in working with his family in running their new financial enterprise. He has redirected his energy, passion, talent, and intellect into managing the assets, building the future for his family, and having a major impact on the causes that matter to him and other family members.

Over the last two years, in collaboration with their family, Stan, Randall, and Rebecca George and her team at LWC, David and Elaine have created, implemented, and now oversee a financial family enterprise. As a result of this process, they have put the following into operation:

- They implemented an aggressive diversification program so that they now hold approximately $50 million in Biocellular stock that represents 20 percent of the overall assets they control.
- They segregated their assets into several investment pools, including their revocable trust, the Singleton Family Investment Partnership, trusts for their grandchildren, and the Singleton Private Foundation.
- The family hired a three-person team to help them manage the operations of their wealth. The team includes chief investment officer Kevin Nolan,* accountant Karen Daniels,* and administrative assistant Cheryl Weaver.*
- They created the Singleton Family board that includes David, Elaine, Kevin Nolan, and two outside board members. The family board oversees management of the entire family enterprise and provides for a governance process to ensure succession to future generations.

- They have funded the Single Family Investment Partnership with $50 million, and through effective leveraged gifting strategies have transferred a $7.5 million ownership interest to each of their four children.
- David, Elaine, and all four children sit on the operating committee of the Singleton Investment Partnership that meets once per month.
- David, his eldest son, Tom, and their chief investment officer, Kevin Nolan, run day-to-day operations of the business.
- Peter, their son-in-law, who has ten years of experience in commercial real estate development, manages the daily operations of the family's real estate portfolio.
- They have set up a family decision-making process and family employment policy.
- They have made over $42 million in direct investments, including co-investment with several private equity firms, venture startups in the biomedical space, social impact investments, and real estate.
- They have created, implemented, and funded the Singleton Family Foundation with approximately $110 million of assets.
- They developed the mission statement for the foundation based an integrated process that included all family members. The foundation focuses on children, healthcare, and the environment.
- David, Elaine, all four children, and their spouses serve on the board of the foundation.
- David, Elaine, and Stacy manage the foundation operations, including screening potential grants and distributing funds to approved organizations and causes.
- They have already made grants to over thirty organizations in excess of $15 million.
- They have set up the structure for a junior board for the grandchildren to participate in grant making when they reach age sixteen and before they are eligible for the foundation board.
- They have conducted two full family retreats focused on education and stewardship. Both events were built around fun with a purpose and engaged all of the generations. Elaine, Gretchen, and their second-oldest son, Trevor, lead the family education and stewardship committees.
- They developed a family website and reporting protocol to keep all family members informed on the current activities of the family enterprise and to plan for future events.

David, Elaine, and Tom left the hospital at 5:30 P.M. All three were feeling sad, excited, and encouraged, all at the same time. Along with meeting with Dr. Delmetro and the hospital board, they had a chance to tour the pediatric cancer ward and connect with some of the kids being treated there. Although it was difficult to see the children facing such challenging and unfair circumstances, they were uplifted by their incredible positivity and perseverance.

As they got into Tom's car, Elaine said, "It's so hard for me to see those kids and know that some of them won't survive to become adults. I know the grant we're making to the hospital might not change things for the children there now, but if we can help save future kids, then we are making a better world."

As they drove out of the hospital through downtown on their way to connect with the rest of the family at Stacy's house for a barbeque, they were eager to share the news of the new cancer center with the rest of the family. Tonight would be a celebration. It would be quite different from David's retirement dinner two years ago at Donovan's. There would be no ties and no speeches, but in many ways it would have more meaning, at least for David.

Index

A

Academy of Achievement, 16
Accounting, tactical aspect,
    107–108
Adults, money management,
    119–122
Advisors
    advisees, relationship, 120
    backgrounds, 44
    compensation, conflicts
        of interest, 45
    engagement, 51
    strategic elements,
        120–121
    tactical issues, 121
Advisory team, impact, 43,
    46
All-hands-on-deck assembly,
    127
*Allison, Mark (case study),
    19–20
American Red Cross, 13
    mission statement, 74
A&P fortune, 9
Asset allocation, 97, 113,
    139–140
    tactical aspect, 107–108
Asset management, 131,
    138–140, 153

B

Bangser, Andrew, 74
Banking, 131, 133–134
    opportunities, 134
    requirements, 134
Beauchamp, Parker, 137
Belonging, sense (promotion),
    92
*Bergmond family (case study),
    27–30
Biltmore, The, 4
Bitterman, Stephen R., 137
Blakely, Sara, 16–17
Bloomberg Advantage, 117
Board membership, candidates
    (suggestions/discussions),
    89
Boston College Center on
    Wealth and Philanthropy
    (study), 18–19
Branson, Richard, 16
Breakers, The, 4
Brier, Marcia C., 118
Budgeting, 121, 132–133
Buechner, Frederick, 100
Buffett, Warren, 16–17
Business
    business-owning family, 73,
    141

Business (*Continued*)
  business-related
      responsibilities,
      absence, 56
  commitment, 103
  enterprise, profile, 43
  executive, transition, 146–152
  growth, 55
  internal machinations,
      100–101
  management, 140–141
    family wealth management,
      separation, 58
  owner family, defining, 73
  planning, 48–50

C
Capital
  long-term
      requirements/short-term
      requirements, 133
  private capital, role, 120
Cash balances, reporting, 134
Cash flow, 121, 132–133
  planning, 131
Caspar, Christian, 72
Chan, Priscilla, 17
Charlize Theron Africa Outreach
      Project, 15
Chase Manhattan Bank, NA, 13
Children
  family history, telling, 63–64
  financial matters,
      education/preparation,
      114–116
  privilege, 34
  venture, example, 36–37

Clemens family (fortune loss), 9
Clients
  client-to-team member ratio,
      43
  experience, 45
  face-to-face communication,
      127
Clifton Strengthsfinder (Gallup
      Press), 105
Coaching (internal and external),
      110
Cole, Suzanne, 94–98
Collaborative decision making,
      empowerment (impact),
      99
Combs, James G., 63
Common interests, regulation, 85
Communication, 101, 123
  client face-to-face
      communication, 127
  electronic communication,
      usage, 127
  impact, 82
  methods, 125–127
  plan, 92, 124
  planning, 7
  protocols, establishment, 85
  rehearsal, avoidance, 128
  skills, 110
  subcommittee, 128–129
Community (family value),
      77
Company
  history, 69
  plans, 147
Compensation models, 42
Conchie, Barry, 105–106

Confidentiality, concern,
   56–57
Conflict
   impact, 94–98
   inevitability, 95
   management, establishment,
      85
   resolution, 81
Connectedness, sense, 63
Consensus, usage, 90
Content, attention, 128
Continuity plans, 85
Continuous improvement,
      culture (building), 113
Control, internal locus, 63
Cooper, Anderson, 5, 114
Cornell University, 17
Corporate ethos, description,
      108
Craig, David, 136
Creativity, tolerance, 103
Credit
   long-term lines/short-term
      lines, 134
   management, 131
Culture, building, 113
CVS, vision statement, 74

D
Daniell, Mark Haynes, 25–26,
      62, 107
DarcMatter, 138
Decision making
   blueprint/problems, 82
   collaborative decision making,
      empowerment (impact),
      99

establishment, 85
framework, building, 72
processes, 139
Deductions, usage, 135
Development programs, creation,
      105
Dias, Ana Karina, 72
Diller, Barry, 17
Direct investment, 140–141
Diversification, 113
   plan, development, 151
   program, implementation,
      153
Due diligence, 45–46
Duke, Marshall, 63
Dunn, Elizabeth, 18
Dyer, Wayne, 15

E
Economies of scale, 55
Economy, improvement, 79
Educational program,
      development, 120
Education, importance,
      113–114
Electronic communication,
      usage, 127
Elstrodt, Heinz-Peter, 72
Embedded family offices,
      55–58
Embedded offices, effectiveness
      (consideration), 58
Emotional intelligence, impact,
      107
Empathy, presence, 110
Empowerment, impact, 99
Ending note, 66

Enterprises
  board, provisions, 89
  exit, example, 100
  operation, 153–154
Entrepreneurs
  family business building, 46
  traits, 103–104
Entrepreneurship, 120
Equities, risk, 137
Estate distribution, example, 53
Estate planning
  family service, 121, 141
  issues, 27
  tactical aspect, 107–108
Ethical choices, 64
Ethical wills, usage, 66
Evaluative mediation, 95
Evans, Janelle, 74

F
FaceTime, usage, 62
Face-to-face communication, 127
Facilitative mediation, 95
Families
  accomplishments, focus, 106
  advisory team, coordination,
    45
  approaches, 30–37
  assembly, 88–91
    duties, 89
  banking requirements, 134
  beliefs, vision statement
    definitions, 73–74
  branches, communication,
    124–125
  business
    building, 46
    expansion, 81
    running, reluctance, 109

bylaws, 85–87
catastrophes, impact, 67–68
collective capacity, leverage,
  26
communication
  domination/planning, 7,
    127–129
  structure, 26
composition, profile, 43
conflict resolution, 81
constituencies, 124–125
constitution, 85–87
  consolidation, 86
continuity service, 141
conversation, perils, 125
council, 88–91
crisis, occurrence, 84–85
decision making, 43, 81
dispersal, 52
education, 8, 113, 117
embedded family office, 56
enterprise, 120
  conflict, impact, 94–98
  informality, impact, 82
entities, complication, 83–84
family business, operation
  (strategic plan/tactics),
  49
fortunes, increase/loss, 9, 79
geographic dispersal, 65–66
governance, 7, 81–85
growth elements, 7–8
harmony, 77
history, 7, 63–65, 120
independence, 51–52
individual family, privacy
  (preference), 51

information, communication,
     63
interests, impact, 106
investment partnership,
     creation (example),
     47–48
investment portfolio, 52, 57
   efficiency/effectiveness,
     increase, 52
journey, question, 72–73
leadership
     development/assistance, 7
leaders, selection process, 76
legacy, 65–68
meetings, 35
   agenda, setting, 91
   arrangement, 98
members, education, 92
mission, 44, 67, 78
narrative, 61–63
needs, 84
operations/policies,
     planning/writing, 92–94
philanthropy service, 141
policies/position papers,
     drafting/revising, 89–90
portals, 126
position papers,
     drafting/revising, 89
purpose, 78–79
recordkeeping, security, 138
resources
   leverage, 26
   managing/sustaining,
     41–42
rights, 88
risk/reward, balance, 8
role clarification, 7

roles/responsibilities, 81,
     120–121
self-governance, 91–92
shared resources, sustaining, 27
stewards, duties, 90–91
stewardship, impact, 26
strategic elements, 120–121
strengths, 58–59
   discovery, 76
structure, disappearance,
     87–88
tactical issues, 121
term, usage, 52
values, 7, 64, 91, 121
   binding, 76
   formalization, 85
   identification, 77
vision, 67, 78, 91, 121
vision/mission, 71, 73–76
   planning, 7
   statements, plan, 67
weaknesses, 58–59
"Family Stories That Bind Us,
     The" (Feiler), 63
Families with Purpose, 78
Family Legacy and Leadership
     (Daniell/Hamilton),
     25–26
Family members
   engagement/inactivity,
     98–101
   local investment opportunities,
     51
   roles, 101
   trusted advisors, usage, 51
Family Office Exchange, 121,
     137
   instivual term, 71

Family offices
  confidentiality, 56–57
  creation/management, 131,
      141–142
  embedded family officers,
      55–58
  involvement, 54
  mistakes, 55–59
  multifamily offices (MFOs),
      52, 55, 141
  questions, 141–142
  requirement, 54–55
  services, 151
  single-family offices (SFOs),
      52, 54–55, 141
Family wealth
  business, 48
  embarrassment, 31
  enterprise, strategic
      plan/tactics, 49
  examples, 27–37
  management, 51, 58
  sustaining, 26
Family Wealth: Keeping It In the
      Family (Hughes), 11
Fee models, 42
Fee structures, conflicts of
      interest, 45
Feiler, Bruce, 63
Financial advisor/planner,
      importance, 132–133
Financial assets, 19–22
Financial capital, 11
Financial decisions, 147
Financial enterprise, running,
      146–152
Financial family, 73
Financial forecasting, 132–133

Financial games, usage, 116–117
Finding Your Roots (Gates, Jr.),
      65
First-generation wealth creators,
      impact, 37
Foley, Henry, 3
Ford Foundation, mission, 75
Ford, Gerald, 13
Ford Motor Company, vision
      statement, 74
Foster, Lauren, 136
Foundation Center, The, 73
Foundation Source, 74
Founding dream, 64
46664, 15
Frank, Robert, 14
Free the Children, 15
Fulfillment, feelings, 20–22
Fun for Kids, 117
Futurewealth Report, The, 126

G
Gallup Press, Clifton
      Strengthsfinder, 105
*Gardenia family (case study),
      68–70
Gates, Bill/Melinda, 16–17
Gates Jr., Henry Louis, 65
Generational differences, 93
Generational shifts, 94
Gilovich, Thomas, 17–18
Giving Pledge, 16–17, 133
Glemser, Anne-Catrin, 109
Global Impact Investing
      Network, 140
Goal direction, 103
Goal-driven data,
      measurement/reporting,
      142–143

Governance
  body, purpose/rules, 85
  documents, usage, 101
  effectiveness, 83
  family governance, 7,
      81–85
  framework, 84–85
  models, impact, 93
  structure
    absence, 84–85
    impact, 121–122
  tools, 72
  types, 91–92
Gray, Lisa, 83, 91–92
Growth, exhibition, 107
Grubman, Jim, 129
Gunther, Robert, 5

H
Hamilton, Sarah S., 25–26, 62,
      107
Hanh, Thich Nhat, 15
Hartford family (fortune
      loss), 9
Hartford II, Huntington
      (business investment), 9
Hawthorn Institute, 73
Health (family value), 77
Health, improvement, 79
Hicks family (multigenerational
      business), 8
High-functioning team,
      interaction, 123
High-level experiential spending,
      pursuit, 17
Howard Hughes Medical
      Foundation,
      purpose/objective, 75
Howell, Ryan, 18

Hughes, James, 11, 19, 49, 94
Human capital, 11
Humanity, promotion of
      well-being, 14

I
ImPact, 14, 17
Impact investment, 106
Inactive members, removal,
      100–101
Individual family
      members, investment
        objectives, 51
      privacy, preference, 51
Information
      management/reporting, 131,
        142–143
      sharing, avoidance, 27
Information technology (IT)
      department, usage, 56
Inheritance, nature
      (understanding), 36
Inheritors, perceptions, 26
Insurance
      deficiencies, 137
      planning, 131
Integrity
      family value, 77
      modeling, 106
Intellectual capital, 11
Intergenerational conversations,
      87
Investment
      education, structured program,
        119
      funds/managers, graduated fee
        schedule, 52
      long-term investment plan,
        113

Investment (*Continued*)
  management, 121, 131,
    138–140
  partnership, example, 152
  philanthropy, 101
  policy, 139
    tactical aspect, 107–108
  strategy (family service), 141
  style, 139
  support, 133

J
Jaffe, Dennis, 77
Jaskiewicz, Peter, 63
Jealousy, impact, 56, 124
"Joys and Dilemmas of Wealth,
  The," 18

K
*Kaufman family (case study),
  30–34
Kennedy family, impact,
  67–68
Kennedy, Fitzgerald, Rose, 67
Kennedy, Joseph P., 67
Kennedy III, Joseph Patrick, 68
Kennedy Jr., Edward, 68
Kennedy, Jr., Robert, 68
Kennedy, Patrick J., 68
Kenyon-Rouvinez, Denise,
  109
Klepper, Michael, 5
Knowledge, flow, 111

L
Law firms, advice (example), 47
Leaders
  actions, 106–107
  issues, 109–110

location, 106–108
  qualities, 108
Leadership
  assistance, 7
  building, 108
  development, 7, 42, 103
  disciplines, 110
  model, development, 26
  potential, assessment, 105
  training programs, 110
  traits, embodiment, 107–108
  values, acid test, 108
Leadership Academy for Girls, 15
Leading, learning process,
  108–111
Learning, culture (building), 113
Legacy, 106, 143, 147
  family legacy, 67–68
  letter, 66
  loss/recapture, 68–70
  recovery, 65–67
Legal actions, example, 30
Lilly Endowment, purpose, 75
Lintz, Kathy, 117
Liquidity, requirement, 139
Listening, importance, 128
Loans, long-term
    lines/short-term lines,
    134
Long-term capital requirements,
  133
Long-term investment plan, 113
Long-term strategy development/
    implementation, 152
Long-term tactical requirements/
    implementation, 152
Long-term wealth preservation,
  94

M

MacArthur Foundation, mission, 75

Mack, Linda, 141

Mahmoud, Shanaz, 57

Management style, impact, 103

Mandela, Nelson, 15

Marble House, 4

Mass Mutual American Family Business Survey, 123

McNees, Pat, 66

*McMillian family (case study) 34–37

Mediation
impact, 95
usefulness, 97

Medicare taxes, payment, 135

Memorial Sloan-Kettering Cancer Center, 13

Mentors, qualities, 111–112

Messages, transmission, 126–127

Metropolitan Museum of Art, 13

Middle-class lifestyle, 28

Miller, Stephen P., 108

Mission, 71, 73–76
family mission, 78
planning, 7

Mission statement
creation, 75–76
development, 154
fluidity, 78
usage, 72
*Mitchell family (case study), 58–59

Monetary lessons, absorption, 119

Money
management, 119
meaning, 120
movement, 134
values, relationship, 116–118

Morehouse College, funding, 12

Multifamily offices (MFOs), 52, 55, 141

Multigenerational businesses, strength, 8

Multigenerational families, wealth, 62

Multigenerational legacy, 125

Multigenerational wealth management, stewardship model, 26

Multiple generations, involvement, 65

Museum of Modern Art, 13

Musk, Elon, 16

Myers-Briggs Type Indicator, 106

N

Natural disasters, 138

Net worth, profile, 43

News, dissemination, 92

Next-generation members, family firm entry, 109

Nixon, Richard, 13

Nonverbals, impact, 125

O

Off-shore investments, 135

Older children, money management, 119

Open-mindedness, tolerance, 103

Oprah Winfrey Network (OWN), 15–16

Organizational/family structure,
    87–88
Organizational structures, 54
    disappearance, 87–88
Organizational tools, usage, 72
Organization, impact, 71
Outside advisors, usage
    (example), 59
Ownership, legal structure, 51

P

Paradise Island, 9
Parents, Kids, and Money Survey
    (T. Rowe Price),
    114–115
Partnership, establishment
    (example), 35
Peace over Violence, 15
Personal beliefs, sharing, 66
Personal fulfillment, 19
Philanthropy, 106, 121, 135
    emphasis, 12–15
Pointers for Parents, 117
Population Council, 13
Postgraduate education/jobs,
    plans, 32
Preisser, Vic, 5
Preparing Heirs
    (Williams/Preisser), 5
PriceWaterhouseCoopers (PWC)
    survey, 82
Private banking, 54, 133–134
Private capital, role, 120
Problem solving, importance,
    94–96
Proprietors
    actions, 27
    perception, 26
Pulitzer family (fortune loss), 9

Q

Qualitative planning issues,
    150–151
Quantitative planning issues,
    150

R

Rainbow Comes and Goes, The
    (Cooper), 114
*Randal family, (case study),
    46–48
Rath, Tom, 105–106
"Representing Family
    Constituencies"
    (Shepherd), 124
Resources, managing/sustaining,
    41–42
Return expectations, 139
Revenue sources, 45
Risk
    appreciation, absence, 137
    factors, 137
    management, 101, 136–138,
        141
    reward, balance, 8
    tolerance, 103, 139
Robbie, Elizabeth, 6
Robbie family, 135
    nonliquid assets, 6
Robbie, Joe, 6
Rockefeller Brothers Fund, 14
Rockefeller Center, 13
Rockefeller, David, 13, 14, 16
Rockefeller III, John D., 13
Rockefeller IV, John D. "Jay,"
    13, 14
Rockefeller, Jr., John D., 12
Rockefeller, Laurance, 13
Rockefeller, Laura Spelman, 12

Rockefeller, Nelson, 13
Rockefellers
    philanthropic discussions, 89
    wealth-building/philanthropy,
        emphasis, 12–15
Role clarification, 7

S
Samuel Bronfman Foundation
    (vision statement), 74
Schiff, Lewis, 116
Schlossberg, Caroline Kennedy,
    68
Schoedinger family
    (multigenerational
    business), 8
Scott, Cynthia, 77
Self-worth, 19
    sense, 20–22
Service models, 42
Shepherd, Sylvia, 124
Sherman Antitrust Act, 14
    Shirtsleeves to shirtsleeves,
        adage, 3
    phenomenon, avoidance, 42
    wealth problem, 113–114
Short-term capital requirements,
    133
Short-term tactical requirements,
    151–152
Single-family offices (SFOs), 52,
    54–55, 141
    expense, 54–55
    Singleton* family 151–155
Skype, usage, 62
Snapchat, 22–23
Social media, proliferation, 62
Soft skills, 107–108
Speaker, concentration, 128

Spelman College, funding, 12
Spiegel, Evan, 22
Spiritual beliefs, sharing, 66
Spirituality (family value), 77
Stakeholders, information
        (provision), 92
Stalk, Jr., George, 3
Standard Oil, benefits, 14
*State of the Art in Family Wealth
    Management, The,*
    137–138
Stein, Helene W., 118
Stewards, 26
    duties, 90–91
Stewardship
    impact, 26
    model, 26
St. Jude Children's Research
        Hospital, mission
        statement, 74–75
Strangers in Paradise (Grubman),
    129
Strategic planning, necessity,
    42
Strategic plan/tactics, 49
Strategic thinking, 105–106
Strategic wealth management
    questions/answers, 43–48
    tactical wealth management,
        integration, 41
Strategic wealth planning,
        elements, 48–50
Strengths Based Leadership
    (Rath/Conchie),
    105–106
Succession plans, 85
Sudden wealth syndrome (SWS),
    signs, 132

T

Tactical issues, strategic
    framework, 131
Tactical skills, presence, 110
Tactical wealth management
    complications, 143
    integration, 131
    questions/answers, 43–48
    strategic wealth management,
        integration, 41
Talent themes, 105
Talking stick, usage, 96
Tax advisors/consultants team,
    136
Tax burdens, 135
Tax compliance, 131, 134–136
Tax planning, 121, 131,
    134–136
    family service, 141
    tactical aspect, 107–108
Tax-reduction strategies, 135
Team-based compensation
    program, offering, 44
Team composition, 44
Team members, compensation,
    44–45
Themint.org (financial
    education), 117
Thomas, Danny, 74–75
ThreeJars (financial literacy
    program), 117
    approach, 120
Tips for Teens, 117
Top-down governance,
    patriarchal style, 91
Townsend, Kathleen Kennedy,
    68

Transaction processing,
    reporting, 134
Transformative mediation, 95
T. Rowe Price, 114
Trusteeship (family service),
    141
Trusts, limitations, 29–30
Turner, Ted (purpose), 16–17
Twain, Mark, 9

U

Ultra-high-net-worth, 34, 43
    clients, 137
Ultra-high-net-worth families,
    41–43, 139
    inheritances, 46
    team, designation, 43
Uncertainty, tolerance, 103
Unity, sense (promotion), 92
USC Marshall School of
    Business, 22

V

Values
    articulation, 66
    creation, 61
    family identification, 77
    family member understanding,
        77
    money, relationship,
        116–118
    values-based strategy, 131
Values Edge System, The
    (Jaffe/Scott), 77
Vanderbilt, Cornelius, 4
    death, 5
Vanderbilt, Frederick William, 4

Vanderbilt, George Washington, 4

Vanderbilt, Gloria, 5, 114–115

Vanderbilt II, Cornelius, 4

Vanderbilts, wealth diminishment, 4

Vanderbilt, William Henry, 4

Vanderbilt, William K., 4

Venture capital firms, employment example, 34–35

Venture capitalism, example, 13

Vision, 71, 73–76

Vision statement
  creation/initiation, 75–79
  expression, 73
  future, 74
  usage, 72
  writing, 76

von Furstenberg, Diane, 17

W

Ward, John, 93–94

Wealth
  advantages, 17–18
  advisors, questions, 142–143
  business, 48
  case study, 19–22
  creation, 61, 64, 81
  creators, 66, 93
  disadvantages, 18–19
  empowerment, 33
  history, 120
    context, 61
  long-term family sustainability, 105

managers, impact, 42

money, comparison, 11

multigenerational families, 62

parent attitude, 118

perspective, alternative, 22–23

planning, strategic dimensions, 48

positive aspects, 116

preservation, 27, 41

problem, 113–114

proprietors, impact, 27

psychological issues, 132

stewardship, impact, 25

team composition, 44

transition, 149

triangle, 19

usage, 33

wealth-building, emphasis, 12–15

Wealth management, 44
  activities, 54
  challenge, 3
  concepts, agreement, 59
  family approach, 51
  future, 146–152
  integrated approach, 43
  integration, 41
  perception, 46
  services, provision, 41
  sustaining, 150

Webinars, usage, 110

What-if cost/benefit analysis, 136

Wiesel, Elie, 15

Williamson, Marianne, 15

Williams, Roy, 5

Willingness, importance, 109
*Wilson, Ken (case study), 53
Winfrey, Oprah, 15–16
Wire transfers, 134
W.K. Kellogg Foundation, vision,
        74
Women for Women
        International, 15
Women in the World
        Foundation, 15
Woolworth family (fortune loss),
        9
World Wealth Report (2015),
        138–139
Written contract, usage, 97

Y

Younger children, money
        management, 119
Yuengling family
        (multigenerational
        business), 8

Z

Zambelli family
        (multigenerational
        business), 8
Zildjian family
        (multigenerational
        business), 8
Zuckerberg, Mark, 17